P9-CEV-555

□■   *The Symbolic and the Real*

BOOKS BY IRA PROGOFF

The Symbolic & the Real

*A New Psychological Approach
to the Fuller Experience of Personal Existence*

Ira Progoff

McGraw-Hill Book Company

New York • St. Louis • San Francisco • Düsseldorf

Mexico • Montreal • Panama • São Paulo • Toronto

The Symbolic and the Real

Copyright © 1963 by Ira Progoff. All rights reserved. Printed in the
United States of America. No part of this publication may be repro-
duced, stored in a retrieval system, or transmitted, in any form or
by any means, electronic, mechanical, photocopying, recording, or
otherwise, without the prior written permission of the publisher.

Library of Congress Catalog Card Number 63-18865

Design: Adrianne Onderdonk

Reprinted by arrangement with The Julian Press, Inc.

First McGraw-Hill Paperback Edition, 1973

07-050892-5

8 9 10   FGRFGR   8 9 8 7

Dedicated to the Memory of

Carl Gustav Jung, 1875-1961

His life and work are a foundation upon which many shall build.

☐ Introduction to the Paperback Edition

In the ten years that have passed since it was originally developed, the program for personal growth that is set forth in *The Symbolic and the Real* has had several extensions of practical importance. Although it is primarily a program for enlarging the life-awareness of individuals, it has been shown in practice to have numerous social applications as well. It has been used, for example, by disadvantaged persons living in urban tension areas; and it has been used by monks living in the quiet of monasteries. Regardless of the differences in external circumstances, the program provides a means by which individuals can connect their lives to deep sources and gain a new personal perspective. Thus it has been able to serve as an instrument of both social and spiritual renewal.

I have often wished during the years when these developments were taking place that I could add an epilogue to *The Symbolic and the Real* to indicate the significant additions that have been made in the basic program. The publication of this paperback edition now gives me that opportunity.

When *The Symbolic and the Real* was first published in 1963, the public attention it received provided me with a much broader range of situations in which to test the methods described and to explore new ones. The new data that was gathered enabled me to make revisions and enlargements on the basic conception, and to tighten the techniques so that they formed an integral approach. Somewhere along the road, the concept and its methodology crystallized into a definite workable unit which was increasingly validated through practice in a variety of cultural situations. This made possible in 1966 the establishment of Dialogue House, which used as the basis of its program the *Intensive Journal* method derived from the formulations presented in *The Symbolic and the Real*. That program has found increasing applications on a national scale to the point where there are now several thousand persons using the registered *Intensive Journal* as the core of their personal disciplines of growth. The practice of the Dialogue House method and of its ongoing program has thus become in fact the living epilogue to *The Symbolic and the Real*.

A central factor of the program originally described in Chapter 5 of this book was a *psychological workbook*. While it contained valuable attributes that are inherent in the nature of journals, it was described here essentially as an unstructured journal. The workbook was to be used in the various relationships that formed the three segments of the program of personal growth: in group workshops, in one-to-one consultations, and in the individual's own privacy. I had used a journal personally and with my clients for many years, and I had found it to be a very helpful tool. This was the basis on which I had included it in the program.

I had found that a journal was especially useful for working with the symbolic material that was produced by the extended experiencing of dreams and images. As experiences of deep symbolism move to the more fundamental levels of the psyche, they tend to become increasingly subtle and elusive. It then becomes essential to have a means of recording them and of working with them.

The recording of dreams is an area of psychological work in which the keeping of a journal is an obvious necessity. While working in the journal with dreams and *Twilight Imagery* experiences, I was however led to realize that there is a further step that can be taken. The use of a journal need not be limited to passive recording; with the correct structure and procedures, a journal can serve as an *active* instrument as well. This realization, which emerged first from my work with symbolic material and was later expanded to all the major contents and processes of a human existence, led to the development of the *Intensive Journal* and the method of *Journal Feedback* in the Dialogue House program.

The expanded use of the psychological workbook as a by-product of the attention given to *The Symbolic and the Real* enabled me to have two important new recognitions concerning its use. The first concerned the limitations that are inherent in an unstructured journal. The second pointed the way to constructive new steps that could be taken to develop a journal whose structure would have a dynamic factor of life-movement built into it. Such a journal could play an *active* role in the growth of persons.

The first of these recognitions was based on observing the fact that when the unstructured workbook was used by the general public and was not limited to people actively engaged in directed psychotherapy, its use tended to diminish and eventually to neutralize itself. I found also that with the passage of time many people tended to fall back into whatever patterns of analytical thinking they had been accustomed to follow. Their minds continued along their usual circular paths, but with the single difference that now they recorded their circles in a journal. Sometimes this even increased the circularity of their experiences, as for example, by reinforcing their tendency to analyze themselves interminably, if that had been their pattern before. It became evident that the mere fact of using an unstructured journal was, by itself, not sufficient. I concluded that it is essential to have a specific methodology that is built directly into the structure of the journal and into the techniques with which the journal can be used.

Understanding this made it clear that the key does not lie in working with a workbook or a journal, but rather in having a *nonanalytical methodology* that reflects harmoniously the creative *Elan* of life as that life-force is moving at the depth of the individual psyche. The basis for such a methodology had already been set forth in *The Symbolic and the Real* in the conception of psyche-*evoking* in contrast with psycho-*analysis*. My main task, therefore, lay in taking the second essential step, that of finding the means to embody this non-analytical method in the structure of a journal. It had to be done, however, in such a way as to build an inner momentum and to draw on factors strong enough to sustain a continuous process of growth. When this further task was achieved, the result was the *Intensive Journal*. It replaced the *psychological workbook* as that had been described in Chapter 5 of this book, and it set the basis for the Dialogue House program.

The details of these further developments in the techniques of personal growth are described in my book on the *Intensive Journal* which is now in preparation. The main concepts and tools of thought that were necessary to create the *Intensive Journal* and the program as a whole are, however, already present in *The Symbolic and the Real*. The basis for the underlying approach can therefore be understood by reading this book. In order to comprehend the concepts fully, however, the reader should be aware that *The Symbolic and the Real* is in fact the culmination of a trilogy of books published between 1956 and 1963. The three books are separate, but also express an inherent unity as they are moving toward a single goal.

The first volume, *The Death and Rebirth of Psychology*, explored the history of depth psychology from Sigmund Freud through Otto Rank in order to identify the ultimate conclusions which these masters reached as the culmination of their lifeworks. Underlying the study was the thought that the well-considered judgments of their last years might provide the starting point for a larger understanding of human experience. I entertained the hope that a new generation could benefit from the errors that had been unavoidably made by the earlier generation of pioneers. In general, that hope has been validated. It has certainly enlarged the perspective in which we can move toward the future. A main result of that study was to show that while depth psychology began with a materialist, psychiatric orientation, the experience of its most creative researchers turned it in the opposite direction moving toward the creative and spiritual potential of human nature. This reversal is what is referred to as the death and rebirth of psychology, and has become the basis for many of the recent developments that have taken place under the name of *humanistic* psychology.

The second and pivotal volume of the trilogy, *Depth Psychology and Modern Man*, used the evolution of the species as the background for developing operational concepts that would both describe the depths of the human person and enable those depths to unfold amidst the pressures of modern civilization. The core structure of a humanistic depth psychology is contained in that book. Published in 1959, it established the integral relationship between the active experience of imagery and the advanced development of human consciousness. On the basis of its interpretation of the process that is involved in the formation of images, it proceeded to a description of creative discovery as that takes place in the life of scientists and other creative artists. Perhaps most significantly, it called attention to the organic ground of man's spiritual life, and to the methods by which new experiences of meaning can be brought into modern existence.

With these two studies as its foundation, *The Symbolic and the Real* focuses on the symbolic dimension of human experience. It discusses symbols not merely as a means of social communication, but as organic expressions of the life process itself. Noting the different types of symbols, especially the distinction between elemental and representational symbols, it turns to the deep contact with the symbolic level as a major source of energy for the revitalization of personal experience.

Beyond the power that is latent in symbols, comparable in the context of the psyche to the energy that is contained in the physical atom, there is also the special quality of the symbolic process that carries the self-balancing wisdom of life. The inherent capacity of the universe to heal and reintegrate itself in its individual parts is made accessible to man through the symbolic dimension. The history of religion contains ample evidence of this, but it also teaches us that an analytic and intellectualistic approach to symbols blocks the capacity of symbols to give us their energy and guidance. For this reason, it is necessary to proceed in a nonanalytic manner if we are to draw the benefits of the depth dimension.

The main thrust in *The Symbolic and the Real* is to provide a nonanalytic approach to the depth dimension so as to draw forth both the energy and the capacity of guidance that is inherent in the elemental symbols. This is the essence of the Socratic method of evoking what is hidden beneath the surface of the human person. It is the principle behind the method of psyche-*evoking,* which is presented here, in contrast with psycho-*analysis.*

The approach of psyche-*evoking* directs our attention

to those levels of human experience that are not directly accessible to our personal, or subjective, consciousness. We are not conscious of them, and to that degree we may say that they are part of the *unconscious*. They are not, however, composed of remnants of repressed past experience, what Freud called the *unconscious repressed* and Jung called the *personal unconscious;* neither do they belong to those half-unconscious levels that condition social behavior and form the realm of the *interpersonal*. Beyond the personal and beyond the interpersonal, the symbols of the depth dimension reflect the organic and the elemental ground of life. They are *transpersonal*.

This term, the *transpersonal,* which has found increasing use in psychology in recent years, plays an integral role in the conceptual framework of *The Symbolic and the Real*. It is the fundamental level of the depth dimension, and refers to the inner space in which the elemental symbols have their effect. It was specifically in order to have a viable method of making regular contact with the transpersonal level of the psyche that the technique of *Twilight Imaging* was developed, as it is described in Chapters 3 and 4. It has been amply validated over the years as an active nondirective means of stimulating and evoking the transpersonal depths of the human person.

Psyche-evoking, both as principle and as methodology, directs itself toward drawing forth the potentials of personality. It does this by proceeding nonanalytically and nondiagnostically, using procedures which, like Twilight Imaging, stimulate at deep symbolic levels the process of growth that is inherent in the human being. It evokes, or draws forth, those potentials within the person that are latent but have not yet been able to be lived. In this way it expands the personal possibilities of what is involved in being human, but it does so at a transpersonal level.

The movement toward a humanistic psychology has implications that reach far beyond the professional field of psychology. It indicates that modern man is now reaffirming his own existence in the dehumanized environment which his technology has created. It is not sufficient, however, for us merely to proclaim that we do indeed exist. It is necessary that we be capable of giving substance to our life; and we can do that by learning to make contact with the dimension of depth that is at the core of our being.

There are levels of reality within us that are much greater than our analytical minds can know. Nonetheless, we can make them accessible to our awareness so that they become channels by which we reconnect ourselves to the great sources of life. Evoking the depths of ourselves is a way to the renewal of our humanity. It is a way, and a method, by which we can become more truly and fully *persons* and by which we can carry ourselves beyond the subjectivity of being merely individuals in a self-seeking world.

Ira Progoff

Dialogue House
New York City
September 4, 1973

☐ Acknowledgments

Some of the ideas used in Chapter I were first presented at the Symposium on American Values at Central Washington State College and have been published in part in Motive Magazine. I wish to express my profound appreciation to the individuals who have graciously permitted me to describe their personal experiences as examples of the depth processes at work in the psyche. Fictitious names have of course been used in all cases. I am indebted to the Foundation for Integral Research in New York City for the use of transcripts of group workshops which I conducted under its auspices.

☐ Contents

1 Towards an atmosphere of growth

THE MISSING RESOURCE

It has been said that the reason our culture does not produce more persons of the quality of Albert Einstein is that we do not really want such individuals in our midst. We feel more comfortable with persons who direct their lives and their work along well-accepted lines. Their actions are much more predictable, and therefore we feel safer with them. We feel protected by reference to statistics, and yet we know that the major breakthroughs of knowledge have their origins in nonrational intuitions that burst unpredictably from the imaginative depths of personality. During the past few years there has been increasing testimony from scientists to indicate that this is so. It has led to the awareness that a major need of the modern community is the development of an atmosphere that will stimulate and nurture the inward growth of creatively visionary persons.

When we consider what can be done to prepare the way so that more unpredictable acts of creativity can happen, we realize that it is not a new method of thought but a special *quality of person* that is called for. We require a style of personality capable of perceiving reality fluidly in the multiplicity of its dimensions. Reality is not limited to the outward form of things, and therefore we require a capacity of vision that can penetrate the opaqueness of tangible experience. This is not merely a mental ability, however. It involves the whole personality in a fullness of sensitivity that perceives more productively in special fields of work because it has a larger relationship to reality as a whole.

The conception of reality in terms of which the individual experiences his life plays a crucial role in setting the possibilities of what a civilization can achieve. That is why one pre-condition for a major development of creative personality in the modern world is an expanded perception of reality beyond the current intellectual boundaries. It is not a question of *ideas* about what is real, but of the relation to reality that an individual can know intimately in the depth and in the fullness of his personal existence. For this, his intellectual philosophy or his conscious attitude is not nearly so important as his *capacity* for recognizing and participating in the varied dimensions of experience. With this capacity well developed, large vistas of experience open to the individual. Without it, the resources for creative insight dwindle and a culture is brought to the situation in which we find ourselves in modern times, living with an abundance of technological facilities but a dearth of persons who are capable of great acts of imagination and of sustained spiritual strength.

The nature of this lack is indicated by the fact that the most important commodity in short supply throughout our culture is imaginative leadership. This is glaringly true of political life, although we live in a time of national and international crisis in which it would seem that herioc capacities would be called forth if they were available. The lack is apparent also in such fields as education, journalism, and the ministry where the standardized images of a mass society neutralize the potentiality of great visions. There are some signs that spiritual life is stirring in the arts. Scientists, aroused by the dangers of the atomic age, have begun to emerge from their laboratories occasionally to speak with the fire of prophets; but even here there is a limitation of personal vista because the experience of reality has not opened to the fullness it requires. Lacking this larger awareness, the major shortage of our culture remains a shortage of human resources, specifically a shortage of persons capable of sustained creative vision together with personal commitment.

Because it is the single most powerful institution in our culture, the business community provides a prime example of this deficiency. The great industrial firms possess ample competence on the level of advanced technical work. There is an abundance of specialized knowledge able to deal efficiently with the intricacies of technology, but the weakness lies on the opposite side. The sensitivity to the inward life of man has remained relatively undeveloped while the material world has been mastered. The result is an imbalance in the psyche of the business community expressing the fact that it has established its superiority on the material realm but has left a vacuum on the other dimensions of human experience. This vacuum is shown in the lack of personal fulfillment within business men individually, and in the general failure of the business world to bring forth men of sufficient inward capacity to step beyond the stereotypes of a materialist culture.

Specifically in the field of business leadership, there is a two-fold problem. A corporate executive has the responsibility of conducting his firm's operations in such a way that they will yield a profit for the stockholders. At the same time, he has a responsibility to the community at large to use the resources of his company in a manner that is conducive to the fuller well being of the civilization that makes the very existence of his company possible. Inevitably a conflict of interest arises here, but it is not the economic conflict that is the chief problem. The primary difficulty lies in the fact that most business leaders, like other members of the community, do not know how they can make significantly valuable contributions to the community, beyond the easy and obvious way of charitable contributions of money. And even if an intimation of such potentials comes to them, they are seldom personally capable of the necessary acts of spiritual responsibility. The habits of thought and action, accumulated over many years in a predominantly materialist society, incline much too heavily in another direction.

It was in recognition of this situation that Chief Justice Earl Warren made his very pertinent suggestion calling for the establishment of a new profession of persons who would advise business leaders on how to use their corporate resources in a manner that is both ethical and culturally valuable.* In making his proposal Justice Warren was expressing the frustration of a sensitive jurist who realizes that for citizens merely to observe the letter of the law is not sufficient. A civilization does not thrive unless its citizens undertake major creative acts of what Pitirim Sorokin has called "altruistic behavior," behavior whose goal is the enhancement of the whole community of man. The problem which must

* See Earl Warren, "The Law Beyond the Law," in *Main Currents in Modern Thought*, January, 1963, Vol. 19, No. 3, pp. 55-60. This is the text of the address in which Justice Warren made his proposal. It was originally delivered at the Louis Marshall Award Dinner of the Jewish Theological Seminar of America, Nov. 11, 1962.

be seen, however, and which we must now find the means to resolve, is that even should leaders in business, the unions, government, and other walks of life learn through their advisors what might be a creative course of social behavior, they would still require the personal capacity of imagination to recognize its implications and to carry it through. It is to this task, I believe, that depth psychology is in a unique position to contribute the means for a solution in our time.

An aspect of this problem, which is one of the important psychological facts of our culture, concerns the emotional life of men who successfully meet the competition and reach a high position in their fields of work. In the business community, for example, the characteristic situation is for a man of ability to attain a top executive level, meeting the challenges of industry with enthusiasm and effectiveness, but to have his personal life dry up in the meantime. While he is concentrating on the cold, objective facts of economic life, the area of the personality in which feelings and beliefs are important wears thin. The consequence is that a man begins to feel, vaguely at first, and soon quite pressingly, that the business activities that used to excite him have somehow become pointless. They are no longer meaningful to him, and he finds himself echoing the phrase of Ecclesiastes, "Vanity of vanities, all is vanity."

This is not merely a question of philosophical outlook, although it may be rationalized in philosophical terms. It is a matter of emotional emptiness and eventually of *ennui* and psychological disturbance. It is expressed in physical ailments, in the search for artificial pleasures, and, more fundamentally, in a feeling of boredom and cynicism that hovers in the background of all personal relationships. It hollows out life, and it has become one of the major problems of modern industrial culture. Stated simply, it is the difficulty of obtaining a sufficient number of men who are capable of functioning creatively in positions of major responsibility once they have beaten the competition and arrived there.

In the practice of psychotherapy, one sees the evidence of this failure in three specific forms: firstly, in the men who reach the higher executive echelons, and then find that it does not hold the meaningfulness which they had thought it promised; secondly, in the number of men in high positions who are counting the years until their retirement; and thirdly, in the emotional confusions, depressions, and disturbances experienced by the wives of such successful men.

There is an especial significance in the number of men who have projected their happiness out of the present situation in which they are living into a future time when they will have retired. These men have reached the point where they believe, or hope, that the meaningful part of their lives will begin after they have completed their active business careers. It is reminiscent of the mythical belief that a golden age will return to the earth one day in some distant messianic time. The more imaginative of these businessmen begin to plan in advance for a new type of work in which they can participate when the fateful day arrives. They hope in this way to avoid falling into a vacuum when the time of retirement begins. In either case, it is clear that their major life work is not meaningful, much less inspiring to them while they are engaged in living it.

The third indication of the emotional problems at high levels in our culture is the number of wives of successful men who require psychological support because of the emptiness they feel in their existence. Both psychologically and culturally, this is a very significant occurrence. In the United States especially, the woman who finds herself in this situation is very often a college-educated, sensitive person who reacts to the fact that the life in which she has been participating vicariously through her husband is not meaningful. It is not meaningful to her because it has no fundamental significance in her husband's life, despite the excitement and tension of the time-consuming activities that it entails.

Usually when such a woman comes for psychological assistance to bolster her emotions, it is really spiritual nourishment that she requires; more specifically, it is the psychological development of her capacities of spiritual awareness that is needed. Most of the time, too, she is just one step ahead of her husband, for she has felt his spiritual need and has interpreted it as a lack in herself. Occasionally it does happen, too, that when she has taken a substantial step toward meaningfulness in her own personal development, this serves a spiritual role for her husband and opens a door for him.

These three types of situation are all indications of a tremendous waste of human resources. It is a waste that occurs because the values of life in the modern industrial culture are too narrow and do not draw forth the larger potentials of personality. It is an urgent problem for our civilization, but we should not expect that the answer to it will be found in new social programs, or in new doctrines and ideologies drawn from the field of religion or politics. Certainly the solution does not lie in a return to the traditional faiths, even if such a return were possible for modern man. It requires a broader atmosphere of belief and experience and especially a freer atmosphere in which the many dimensions of reality can be more fully known.

The great need is to enlarge not only the awareness of reality but to enlarge the capacity of experiencing its deeper levels in the symbolic terms it requires. Our task in the pages that follow is to explore the psychological conceptions and the psychological techniques that will make it possible to establish such an atmosphere in modern culture and to increase the sensitivity of individuals to the ground and source of creativity.

What is involved in an *atmosphere?* If we were fish, our atmosphere would be water. As land animals, our atmosphere is air. In this sense, an atmosphere is that in which a species lives and moves and has its being. The atmosphere provides the background as well as the main ingredients, the possibilities and the limitations of a species' life.

When we think of the atmosphere of the human being, however, we notice something different. The atmosphere of sea animals and land animals is external to them; it encompasses them physically as they move around in it. The primary atmosphere of human beings, however, is not outside of them physically. It is within them psychologically. It is to be found in their attitudes toward their deepest assumptions about the nature of existence, and their underlying feelings regarding themselves and their fellowmen.

The primary atmosphere in which the human being lives and moves and has his being is inward. It is contained in the way a person thinks about himself, perceives and experiences his fundamental nature. It involves his conception of himself, his potentialities, and the resources upon which he can draw. These comprise the atmosphere of his life, and they are within him. But they are not only internal individually; they are within the depths of persons in a way that reaches across the community. The inward atmosphere of a civilization is a social fact that is expressed psychologically in the individuals who comprise the culture. The task of improving the quality of a civilization must therefore be approached in terms of the individual in the culture and his personal experience of meaning, or lack of meaning, in life.

In modern times, depth psychology is that particular discipline which undertakes to provide the methodology and the techniques by means of which an experience of meaning and of spiritual contact can become an actuality. Many people are in favor of an experience of meaning, and they speak philosophically or sociologically in support of it, emphasizing its importance for human existence. The difficulty, however, is that merely to be in favor of meaning in human existence does not make the knowledge of it a reality. It becomes then a wish that is intellectually supported but is not a fact of experience. To make it possible psychologically for modern persons to experience meaning in their lives, more than a philosophy or a theology is required. A psychological methodology is called for, and it is to this task that modern depth psychology directs itself.

In my consulting work people often come and tell me that they feel that they are neurotic and frustrated because there is no meaning in their lives. They feel that if they could know the meaning of life, their psychological functioning would be much more productive. They would like me to give this knowledge to them, but of course I cannot do that. There is no use in one person attempting to tell another person what the meaning of life is. It involves too intimate an awareness. A major part of the meaning of life is contained in the very process of discovering it. It is an ongoing experience of growth that involves a deepening of contact with reality. To speak of it as though it were an objective knowledge, like the date of the war of 1812, misses the point altogether. The meaning of life is indeed objective when it is reached, but the way to it is by a path of subjectivities. It requires a series of profound experiences within the privacy of the personality. The meaning of life cannot be told; it has to *happen* to a person. And a knowledge of the nature and principles of the deep psyche is valuable in helping it to happen.

One of the reasons that one person cannot tell another the meaning of life is that in modern times there is so little common framework of discourse in which the ultimate questions of existence can be discussed. The traditional context of beliefs has lost its relevance for large segments of the population. One cannot merely appeal to old doctrines, nor even to the symbolic language of the Bible. It is not that the insights of traditional religion are not true; it is simply that their relevance and meaningfulness is not felt strongly enough in the modern situation of life to be psychologically effective.

For many reasons in a culture that is dominated by technology and commerce, people have fallen outside the spheres of influence of beliefs that are traditional in Western civilization. We may not approve of this situation at all and strongly deplore it because of the serious psychological and social consequences it has; but it is a fact nonetheless. If we are seriously and sincerely concerned to make it possible for modern man to experience meaning in his life, we must begin by taking this fact into account. It means, specifically, that when we approach the psychological task of developing a method of reaching through to the central experience of selfhood, we require a method that does not depend upon assuming a belief in any special traditional symbol. Eventually many persons may return to the traditional contexts of beliefs, in old or in new forms; but the methods by which they renew their capacities of recognizing meaning in life cannot begin by appealing to those symbols. We have to begin with something neutral, with the psychological condition as it exists at any given moment in the life of the individual. Thus, in order to achieve the new atmosphere of awareness that our time requires, we have to refer not to doctrines or beliefs but to facts of experience, to inward events as modern persons can know them. This is why our primary source material in the pages that follow is drawn from the psychological encounters of modern individuals.

BIOLOGY, HISTORY, AND THE MEANING OF LIFE

The need for a human experience of meaning is one of the most striking phenomena in the world of nature. As far as the present state of science permits us to understand it, man has emerged from a large process of biological evolution; but he is drawn by an aspiration that reaches beyond it. It is as though man's nature requires him to transcend himself, to strive ever to leap over his own evolutionary head, and to live his life not only in its limited and immediate context but in relation to the fullness of the universe. There are important implications in this that science has still to explore.

Perceptive biologists have marked off certain basic facts in this connection. Ludwig von Bertalanffy has pointed out that the human organism does not fulfill even its essential biological functions when it does not feel a framework of meaning.* The basic life processes break apart when they are not cohered by beliefs in a larger purpose.

In a similar vein, Edmund Sinnott † has called our attention to the fact that the unfoldment of inherent patterns of meaning, varying with the species and the environmental circumstances, is a basic process of life. When these patterns of meaning break down so that a purpose is no longer felt in life, the organism loses its will to live and its functioning deteriorates. We have seen that amply demonstrated historically in the way that primitives have lost their elan of life when their rituals were effectively prohibited by governments so that the primitives were left to conclude that their gods

* Ludwig von Bertalanffy, *Problems of life,* New York, Harper Torchbooks, 1960, and *Modern Theories of Development,* New York, Harper Torchbooks, 1962.

† Ira Progoff, *Depth Psychology and Modern Man,* New York, Julian Press, 1959, Chap. V, "Biology and depth psychology: the perspectives of Edmund Sinnott."

either had died or had lost their power. We have seen it also in the modern world where the breakdown of traditional beliefs has resulted in social confusion and in disorders of personality.

There is a close interrelationship between biology and human culture. When the cultural milieu provides a system of values and beliefs that is readily accepted by the members of the community, there is a substantial feeling of meaning in life, and the individuals in the culture function well. No matter how primitive the culture may be, when a cultural framework of beliefs is strong enough to provide a purpose in existence, the individuals function well within the limits of their culture. They may not be living in terms of the larger dimensions of "truth," but they are at least able to function effectively with a minimum of breakdown physically and emotionally. When this social context of meaning is lost, the incidence of illness among individuals, both physical and mental illness, rises sharply.

This, in fact, is the historical background against which depth psychology was first developed in modern Europe in the nineteenth century. At that time the traditional frameworks of meaning in Western civilization had broken down and individuals no longer possessed secure guideposts to guide them in the basic activities of their lives. In the old framework, for example, your marriage was arranged for you, or you knew at least what kind of marriage relationship you would eventually enter. You knew largely what the sexual mores required; you knew how you would spend Sunday; you knew with a fair amount of definiteness what constituted moral and ethical behavior. But when those traditional standards broke down—and I am not by any means suggesting that it was not historically necessary for them to break down in order that a larger awareness of reality might develop in modern times—there followed a period of confusing flux in beliefs regarding the social and spiritual meaning of life. Its outcome was a major increase in the functional illnesses to which human beings are susceptible, psychogenic illnesses both physical and mental.

The great contribution of Sigmund Freud's work lies in his medical perception of the psychological effects of this cultural breakdown of values in the nineteenth century. He recognized and described how malfunctions develop in the personality, physically and psychosomatically. As a medical man Freud had no alternative but to interpret what he saw in the light of pathology. He looked for diagnosis and approached the subject as a medical man would approach other physical-medical problems. He took the sexual problems which he observed more or less at their face value, not recognizing the implications of the fact that they were by-products of a cultural transformation. Interpreting the nineteenth century confusions regarding sexual mores as his basic psychological fact, Freud developed the concept which in an enlarged form became the cornerstone of modern depth psychology, the conception of the unconscious.

The problem which set the background against which psychoanalysis was developed was created by the breakdown of a context of meaning in European culture. Psychoanalysis as Freud constructed it undertook to solve the problem in medical terms. Experience with psychoanalysis over the past half century has increasingly shown, however, that one cannot reach an experience of meaning by following an approach of diagnostic analysis. What is required is a method of drawing psychological experience forward, or drawing it onward. In the new, emergent approach, depth psychology becomes a discipline that works toward the development of the personality as a whole. Its primary goal can no longer be adequately stated in terms of medical therapy for it directs itself not to the analysis of pathology but to the *evoking* of larger realizations of meaning in the individual's existence. This defines its style of approach. Significantly, however, though medical therapy is not its primary goal, we find that psychological work directed toward evoking the fullness of potentiality in the person has an especially releasing and invigorating therapeutic effect.

The material of depth psychology is difficult to communicate because its symbolic experiences elude intellectual statements. If, for example, one were seeking to set forth a philosophy, he would proceed by describing the concepts involved. If he were interested in presenting a body of theoretical knowledge, he would likewise proceed by presenting the assumptions, describing the evidences, and move toward his conclusions in logical terms. He would thus analyze, delineate, and communicate his position by means of intellectual ideas. In depth psychology, however, the primary material to be communicated is not contained in intellectual ideas but is a quality of experience. Its essence is a tone of feeling, and this is something that a flat statement of concept and idea cannot convey.

In general it is correct to say that in describing and communicating the material of depth psychology we work our way to concepts by means of metaphors. Alfred Adler made the remark many years ago that "man knows more than he understands." With these words he was calling attention to the fact that, while our knowledge of the world is worked out primarily by means of the intellect, man possesses a capacity of knowledge that operates by something other than rational procedures. If intellect and reason can be spoken of as operating on the "surface" of the mind, this other aspect of cognition is *deeper;* it is beneath the surface of consciousness. It is difficult to find the right word to describe this capacity of knowing which Adler described as greater than understanding. It may be spoken of as intuition, as subliminal, or as paraconscious cognition; but regardless of the term that is used, it is clear that the existence of a capacity of cognition that functions in man beneath the surface of his mind is a fact to be recognized, investigated, and applied.

To speak of this aspect of the psyche is difficult, and

yet we must devise concepts for discussing it and methods for working with it. When we speak of the *levels* of conscious and unconscious, we must understand that we are using the conception of *depth* only in a metaphoric sense. It should never be taken literally. This metaphor of depth has provided a most fruitful context of thought ever since Freud began to think in terms of the strata of the unconscious. Freud however approached the depth of personality in terms of the concept of *repression*. This is the idea that a human being living in society has certain urges and memories which he cannot bear either to express or to remember, and therefore he *represses* them. Once they are repressed, according to Freud's interpretation, they drop into the unconscious where they are transformed so that they are no longer expressed in their direct literal form but are symbolized. Freud's insight into this phenomenon provided the basis for his analysis of the pathology of the mind.

In contrast to this conception, the other metaphoric approach to studying the unconscious is in terms of a natural process of growth at the depth of personality. The metaphor that is most appropriate here is that of the seed. In the seed there is the latent potentiality of development that carries all the possibilities of what the full grown species can become. Following this metaphor, the fullness of the oak tree is latent in the acorn. It is implicit there, and correspondingly, the depths of man, his *unconscious*, is the carrier of human potentialities.

It contains the possibilities of human development that are present in the individual but are not visible because they have not yet become manifest in life. We cannot see them until they begin to unfold and fulfill themselves in the world. For this, it is necessary that the individual develop the capacity of perceiving the inward process of his growth while it is still in motion and before it is fulfilled. As he becomes sensitive to it and attunes himself to the process of his growth inwardly, he is able to draw his potentialities forward. To provide the methodology for this is a primary task of depth psychology.

As a result of Freud's original conception of the unconscious, the conception of *symbol* holds a particularly important place in depth psychology theory. The later development of the understanding of the unconscious, however, especially in the work of C. G. Jung as his work has led to an awareness of the seed principle of potentiality, has made it particularly important to recognize the distinction between the nature of *symbols* when they serve an inherently symbolic role and when they function merely as *signs*.*

Freud's conception of the repressed aspect of the unconscious centers on his statement that when memories or wishes are repressed they are transformed into symbolic terms. It seems more accurate, however, to speak of these not as symbols but as signs because the sense

---

* See the important distinction between Elemental Symbols and Representational Symbols in Chap. III, Section 3, below. p. 89.

of his conception is that if dreams have a specific meaning the content of the dream stands for something else which is the real experience behind the dream. In contrast to this, a bona fide *symbol* does not refer to a specific object of past experience or to a specific wish as when a dream replaces one object and represents it by another. Rather, a symbol appears as a spontaneous image which emerges from the depth of the personality and acts as a vehicle by which the potentiality latent in the unconscious of the individual can be carried forward. The symbol embodies the open future as that future is becoming the present in the seed-depths of the individual. It provides the motive force by which this potentiality can unfold and become actual in the world.

In this perspective, it seems most inadvisable to approach a symbol in an analytical way. If we reduce it to experiences of the past, we deprive it of its potentiality. It results in a major error of interpretation because the symbol, as a factor of unfoldment, does not really have its origins in the past experience of the individual any more than the potentials of an egg are drawn from the past experience of the chicken it is about to become. To break it apart and analyze it would deprive it of its power for life. The more productive way to approach a symbol is to work with it affirmatively, to encourage it, nurture it, and draw it forward. If we nurture it properly, the symbol will open as naturally as a bud. By means of it, then, the process of individual growth can proceed, moving through the symbol which functions as the active psychological medium of personal development.

ANXIETY AND OUR SOCIAL OPPORTUNITY

The forward-moving quality of personality is expressed ultimately in the acts and events of an individual's life. These are the outcome of the factors of potentiality that unfold in the depth of the psyche. The source of outward events lies on the symbolic level of personality, especially in the flow of imagery that constitutes the transrational ground of the mind. We shall discuss the principles of this in detail in Chapter III, but here some dream examples can give a foretaste of the quality of personal experience that is integral to the growth of personality.

In a group workshop in which we were exploring the principles of the psyche by using our personal material, one of the participants told a dream that is characteristic of the psyche in transition. This young man was a graduate student who had experienced one difficulty after another in his life. He would start one line of activity, carry it forward, then stop it arbitrarily. He would start another course of action, then another, develop each to a point, then feel impelled to cut it short and begin something new. In his frustration he was becoming convinced that a fixed pattern was operating in his personality, that it would cause him to ricochet throughout life, and prevent him from ever harvesting the results of his labors. Finally, at a point of personal crisis, he had the following dream.

In the dream he was at a large party where a game was being played in which everyone was required to go on a treasure hunt. The dreamer left to take part in the hunt in the company of a group, but there was the feeling in the dream that to find the treasure was his particular task. In the course of their hunt they came to a misshapen tree. As they approached it they noticed that on one of its twisted limbs there hung a shiny key. It was bright and golden, and they knew immediately that the treasure they were seeking was to be found directly beneath that key.

Quickly someone in the group obtained a shovel and the dreamer began to dig. He had time to dig one or two shovelfuls when the ground suddenly opened. It opened of itself, very wide and deep, enabling them to see far down into the depths of the earth. There the dreamer glimpsed an object which he immediately recognized to be the hidden treasure. He could see, however, that in order to reach it, a tool much larger than the shovel would be necessary. The members of the group realized that more work would have to be done before they could get access to the treasure, and so they went off to obtain the additional tools. When they had gone a short distance, they stopped and looked back at the tree. Now they observed that the deformed tree was not misshapen any more. It had become tall and straight and was standing before them pleasant to their sight. As this realization of the transformation of the tree was breaking in upon the consciousness of the dreamer, the dream ended and he awakened.

When a dream like this is related, a first question concerns the quality of feeling that accompanies it. In this case, the dream carried both an atmosphere of tension and an indication that a new perspective was opening for the dreamer. It seemed to be summing up his past experiences with respect to their meaning for his future. His life was described as a misshapen tree, and the movement of the dream indicated a sequence of events by which the nature of this tree would change. It brought him the insight that the guidance he required would be forthcoming precisely because of the mistakes and distortions involved in his previous experiences. The shiny key was hanging on the misshapen tree. It was necessary that he perceive the misshapenness of the tree, and that he recognize that this was the marker of the treasure he was to find.

The dream showed him also the relation between the key and the treasure, pointing out the importance of looking below. The next crucial step was that he actually get to work and begin to dig toward the treasure. Once he had started the work, once he had broken ground by his own efforts, the work could be carried forward for him more expeditiously by forces greater than himself. It somehow happened of itself. As he was leaving, he realized that the nature of the tree itself had changed in the course of his efforts. This further verified the assurance he had received regarding the future when he looked into the chasm where the treasure was hidden.

A dream like this reveals a great deal concerning the nature of the process working at the depths of personality. As the tension resulting from frustration builds within the person, an intensity of awareness seems to generate in the psyche focused on the present moment as a great *now* of immediate experience. The *now* becomes intense and expansive, reaching backward in time, forward into the future, and presenting itself as a mid-point in the movement of life. It thus provides a dynamically balanced perspective of the unfolding life of the person as a whole.

Dreams that are born of this intensity are incisive in their apt descriptions and broad in the vistas they present. They crystallize the past in an image, as the image of the misshapen tree, and they use the intensity of *now* as leverage for a sensitive leap into the future. The individual who is able to recognize such a dream and respond to it draws from it a strong feeling of where he is in the present moment of his life, and an intimation of how the future can be approached in order that the seed of potentiality may unfold.

This dream of the treasure hunt expressed a great tension, but the anxiety connected with it was not of an intensity great enough to upset the equilibrium of the person. When anxiety reaches that point, the situation becomes much more serious. It then presents much greater difficulties to work with, and is certainly much less pleasant to live through. Paradoxically, however, and precisely because of the disturbance it involves, severe anxiety opens an even greater opportunity for growth in relation to the depths of the psyche.

A good instance of this larger growth is expressed in the process of development experienced by Gregg, a commercial artist. Gregg began his psychological work because of a dream that carried so great an anxiety that it aroused a fear in him that he was going insane. It was a fear, to be sure, that he had felt from time to time over a period of years, but the nightmare quality of this particular dream convinced him that his situation had become especially precarious.

The action of this dream took place at a summer resort. Gregg was strolling on a boardwalk as were many other vacationers, browsing among the amusement places or having tea in outdoor cafes. Everything was relaxed and pleasant when suddenly the tide began to rise. It went higher and higher until it seemed that the water would reach the boardwalk on which the vacationers were strolling. Large tidal waves began to roll over the beach and onto the boardwalk. The concrete supports of the boardwalk began to sink into the sand and to buckle under. Large holes began to open in the boardwalk. People were screaming in panic and the tidal waves were becoming larger and more frequent. It seemed that all would be inundated, and Gregg awakened from the dream in a condition of overpowering anxiety convinced that the forces of the unconscious were about to sweep his sanity away.

How might one approach a dream that carried such serious implications? Our first task was to enable Gregg to become calm enough to collect his emotions so that he could get his bearings in life. For this, we needed to experience the dream anew in a manner that would enable him to feel its place in the movement of his psyche as a whole. We discussed the intensity of emotion that had accompanied the dream and Gregg's feelings indicated strongly that something of major proportions was at work within him. There was indeed a severe agitation in the depths of the psyche. The tidal wave was a sign that an irruption was taking place which would disturb ever larger and deeper segments at the submerged levels of personality.

One of the results of this disturbance was bound to take the form of dreams and visions that would be strange and elusive in their symbolic style. This would be so because unused portions of the psyche would be aroused and drawn out of the darkness into the range of consciousness. We could therefore anticipate that the dream of the tidal wave would be but the precursor of a series of dreams that would be increasingly strange and increasingly profound in their symbolism. This would be a measure of the deepening of the disturbance. It was an indication too that the turmoil in the depth was activating dormant symbols of great power.

As these would unfold through dreams and visions and Gregg's art works, they would become a channel for the principle of integration. This is inherent in human personality. The turmoil of symbols would be brought forth in the midst of anxiety and would eventually bring an awareness of meaning in life to which the individual had not had access before.

In this perspective we could see that while the threat of psychic inundation in the dream indicated a clear and present danger, it also presented a rich opportunity for larger personal development. In the midst of a most precarious situation, the disturbance in the depth of the psyche was making available to the personality as a whole a resource of symbolic mental contents which would progressively provide the raw materials for a fuller experience of selfhood. As we proceeded in the work we did indeed discover that an important aspect of Gregg's problem was his feeling that major potentials in his psyche were remaining unlived. He felt this vaguely and heavily as a frustration of his life energies and he sensed that the anxiety which was enveloping his personality was connected with the fact that a large part of his nature was remaining unfulfilled. Capacities of awareness and of art which were latent in him were remaining unlived. The question which arose in our work was how these could be stirred to life so that they could become accessible to the growing person.

The deep disturbance expressed in the dream

showed the way to the answer. It was itself the beginning of the answer, provided that the proper attitude
could be followed. The tension which produced the
dream did so by disturbing, deep in the psyche, images that had lain quiescent over the years. It aroused
the great energy latent in them; and in this lay both the
danger and the opportunity. The waters rising from
the deep psyche as they appeared in the dream could
very possibly inundate the personality, as the dreamer's
anxiety led him to fear they would; or these same waters expressing the depth of the psyche could become
the supplier of major additional resources for the expansion of his creative life.

In such a situation, the best way of proceeding would
seem to be to draw the movement of the psyche further
on, not to try to push back the ocean, but to encourage
it to flow onward as much as it would. We should not
turn against it, to break it down by analysis and thus
deprive the process of its momentum. Rather we should
cultivate it, seek to evoke it still more fully, and establish a sympathetic relation with it. If we learn to feel
its inner rhythm so that the psyche as a whole is able
to *go with* the disturbance in a harmonious way, it becomes possible for the potentialities which have been
lying dormant to come forth and unfold in life.

In working with Gregg, the movement of dreams was
encouraged, and they continued at ever greater depth.
After a while, as the process of symbolic unfoldment

had established itself, we came to a particular experience that marked a turning point.

Gregg awakened one night from a dream with his customary anxiety symptoms, but there was an additional sensation accompanying it. He felt that he was experiencing the inner rhythm of the encompassing process of disturbance and growth through which he was living. In that moment the rhythm of it seemed to stand apart from him as though it were some abstract principle of nature, as though it were as objective a fact as the movement of his blood within him or the natural healing of a cut upon his skin. He felt that he was not identified with the anxiety. Suddenly he felt that he had been set free. The anxiety was there, but in that moment it seemed to have been separated from him. He still felt it, but he was freed from its possessive power.

Relaxing then, Gregg lay back upon his pillow and used a therapy technique we had used before, the technique of *twilight imaging*.* He closed his eyes and, pretending that a screen was there before his mind's eye, he permitted images to pass before him on the screen. First he had an image of a great frog standing upright and emerging from the surf with a huge egg in its mouth. He felt this image to be a token of a transformation taking place within him, and as he did so the frog changed into a handsome young man who seemed to

---

* See Chap. IV for a description and further illustration of this method.

glow. The radiance surrounding the figure made it a tremendously reassuring image.

Presently a second image came. It was simply a piece of lettuce, flawed at the center by several large brown spots. Beside the lettuce leaf there was a scissors. No one was holding it, but the scissors was cutting towards the brown spots in the center of the lettuce. In the image he said, "Oh, I know what that is. The scissors are going to cut out the bad parts." As he thought this, however, the scissors stopped. He understood this too, and he said to himself in the image, "Oh, I know why that is. That's because I became conscious of it. Now I'll relax and not be conscious of it." He did that. He became quiet, drew his attention away, and the scissors began clipping away again and cut the brown spots out. He recognized the implications of these images and understood the perspective they were bringing him. They became a guiding symbol for him in his life, as they can be for anyone who is engaged in creative work.

The experience that was carried by this series of images became a turning point in our consultations. Though the images were not directly concerned with the personal problems that beset him, the contact which they brought with the underlying principle of the psyche made it possible to meet these personal problems with a more-than-personal perspective. From that point onwards, we were able to achieve our therapeutic goals more directly. The experience had opened the way for a steady enlargement in the capacities of his personality, and for a growing awareness of meaning in his life.

What does such an experience of contact involve? By means of it a person discovers his intimate connection with a principle that works within him and sustains an active, effective process in his psyche. Before the experience of it had happened to him personally, he could talk about it. He could describe it, call it to the attention of the individual, and praise it. But to be in favor of it is of no consequence if one has not encountered it as a living truth that is available to him. It is necessary that it be felt and known as a reality of life; and for this an experience is required, an experience by which its actuality becomes concrete as a fact of intimate knowledge in the person.

To permit this to become real, a certain passage of time is required. One can recognize what is valid in it and agree with it verbally in an instant. One can achieve an understanding of it in as short a time as is required for intellectual insight to transpire. But this will not suffice. An inner knowledge of the principle behind the process is required; and this can come about only with enough time to permit the cycles of the psyche to deepen the level of awareness in the midst of tension and anxiety. It is necessary, too, that the individual commit himself to the process, that he sensitize himself to the style of the nonconscious psyche, and that he follow its path in his dreams and imagery. As he continues with it, not knowing its duration in advance but remaining true to it nonetheless, a point comes at which it culminates and opens as though of itself, in a manner similar to the separation from the anxiety in the imagery we have described. Then a subtle dimension of awareness is touched, the inner principle of it is known directly, and a new quality of existence is felt to be real and encompassing.

The point of contact at which this happens becomes a turning point in the individual's experience because he enters a totally different, psychological atmosphere when it occurs. He perceives the world in radically altered dimensions and the relation between his personal existence and the universe around him is transformed.

The outer context of his life does not immediately change, but the inner context changes fundamentally, and this is the crucial aspect. It indicates to us the special quality of *atmosphere* where human beings are concerned. The effective world in which we move is an inward world. It encompasses us from within our psychological natures by setting the tone and framework for the patterns of behavior which we enact in the world. The dimension of reality that we perceive and experience most intimately is the *effective atmosphere* of our lives, and the transformation of this atmosphere is the key to successful therapy at a deep psychological level.

When the psychological atmosphere in which an individual is experiencing his life is characterized by so-

cial pressures and environmental competitiveness, he is
at the mercy of anxieties. These anxieties arise within
him and they take over his life from the inside; but
their origin lies in the fact that the primary atmosphere
of his existence is defined by environmental factors. He
perceives himself in outward terms. Only at the point
where he experiences himself in terms of the dynamic
factors working and unfolding within his psyche can
the atmosphere of his life change sufficiently to alter
the functioning of his personality. When he has encountered the inward principle working in the psyche
and when he has recognized it as the effective power of
his being, the framework of his experience alters and he
can perceive the world in a new context. With this he
becomes capable of meeting his anxieties and overcoming them by means of a superior inward power.

On the level of personal psychology, this quality of
experience with its consequent change in awareness has
a strongly therapeutic effect. There is an even broader
aspect to it, however. It opens access to a resource
within the personality from which the individual can
draw new materials for his life. It serves as a new source
of insight for him, a new source of ideas and inspira-
tions and meanings. He has touched, in other words,
the deep psychic fount of creativity within man. He
may have heard about it before; he may have wistfully
wondered about it before; but when the encounter with
the deep and dynamic principle of the psyche occurs,

he knows it to be a fact. He can then enter and live in a new atmosphere of awareness.

We may agree that by means of the processes to which we have referred it is possible to establish an atmosphere of growth in the psyche of a modern individual; but what shall we say of the social atmosphere as a whole? Modern culture is predominantly outerori-ented. Its dominant values are personal competitive-ness, conspicuous consumption, status climbing, and the like. More important, and related to this, is the fact that the primary terms for its perception of reality are sensory and materialistic. They are materialistic not merely in the general sense of accepting the objective importance of sensory data; for this is essential in the broadest terms for the individual's adaptation to life as well as for the empirical work of science. But they are materialistic in the more specific sense of the *atti-tude* that is adopted in valuing and judging life ex-periences. In this outlook, the dynamics of the outer world are felt to be of much greater importance than the dynamics of the inner world, which are often dis-missed as vague, fuzzy, and rather unreal. This par-ticular form of materialism, which is the attitude that rejects the reality of the inward, sets the terms in which individuals experience and enact their lives in much of modern culture.

The psychological consequences of living in this so-cial atmosphere are inevitable, and we see them all around us in this period of history. Not perceiving and not being connected to the inward principle of growth, the modern individual has no protection against the anxieties that come upon him as a result of the pressures of his competitive environment. Only if he makes the inward connection in the depth of the psyche can he establish a new atmosphere that will protect him and sustain him. He will then both protect himself against anxiety and connect himself with the sources of creativity.

Both on a personal level and on a social level, the importance of strengthening the capacities of inward contact is coming to the fore in our culture. This is the larger significance of the suggestion made by Justice Warren that a new profession of ethical counselors be established. It is more than standards of ethical conduct that are involved. The great need is for a profession of counselors capable of drawing forth from the depths of individual personality a richer sensitivity to the potentialities of life in large numbers of modern persons, and especially among those who hold responsible social positions.

This means a class of counselor that can serve as an *evoker of persons.* His tools will be psychological, but his goals will reach far beyond psychotherapy in its limited clinical sense. His task will be not to instill moral values by didactic preachments, but to open a way of personal experience that will validate itself integrally and uniquely in the intimate depths of each individual.

The ethical conduct of life in our civilization can then be altered on the basis of these experiences, and be illuminated by the enlarged awareness of reality which they bring.

Such a profession of counselors, working as evokers of personal growth, could well check the tide of moral decay and personal meaninglessness that is rising in our culture. In addition to bringing an effective therapy for anxiety, they could restore to us the missing resource of personality that our time in history requires. But no group of people can function in a vacuum. They require a social atmosphere that is conducive to their style of work, that appreciates its meaning, and that supports it. Most of all, they require a perspective of knowledge, tools, and a methodology with which to carry out their tasks; to provide a basis for this is the primary purpose of this book. In the chapters that follow we shall seek to set forth a perspective of theoretical concepts and practical procedures with which the great social and psychological enterprise of our time can be pursued. A work of individuals and of groups is called for in order that a new atmosphere of reality be established in our time.

We have the task of developing an atmosphere for creativity in our modern culture on two levels. Firstly, on the social level, we require an attitude that affirms the importance of the inward life and sees it as a legitimate and valuable concern, especially for persons engaged in the tough-minded pursuits of industry and science that characterize our world. Secondly, on the personal level, we need to provide situations, information, and a program of practice that will enable a significant number of individuals to reach through to the dimension of depth in human existence, to encounter the reality of inward truth, to recognize its power and meaning, and to validate this larger knowledge as a fact of personal experience. As a basic first step, if we can learn to feel at home, to wander about, to explore, and to discover in the dark and mysterious atmosphere of the depths of the psyche, we shall have access to the psychological resources that we need in order to turn the anxieties of our time into a major opportunity.

2 Psyche-evoking for our time

SOCRATES AS EVOKER

When Socrates was called before the court in Athens to speak in his defense, he presented a statement of the meaning of his personal existence that has the greatest significance for the psychological situation of modern man.

Socrates there described his intimate feeling of why it was important for him to live his life as he had been living it. It was not a question of an intellectual philosophy, but of a *calling* that came to him from two sources, an outward source and an inward source, which Socrates understood as ultimately not separate at all from one another. The outward source of his calling was the *gods* of the Greek Pantheon; and to this the Oracle at Delphi testified. The inward source of his calling was the oracle within himself. He described this as "the divine faculty of which the internal oracle is the source." To Socrates the inward and the outward were two aspects of a single principle. It was in the light of this unity that he could state his belief "that there are gods in a sense higher than that in which any of my accusers believe in them."

The calling which became Socrates' way of life was not something he had deliberately chosen after careful rational thought. He had simply found himself to be living that way, and only afterwards, from the statements of the oracle and from his own examination of himself, he eventually recognized the unplanned path his life had taken. This was why when Socrates had to deliver before the court the speech on which his fate would depend, he felt it to be inappropriate to deliver a speech that had been written in advance. He would use only "the words and arguments which occur to me at the moment," since that manner of speech alone would be true to the manner in which the vocation of his life had unfolded.

He had become aware of his special role almost by chance. An Athenian, Chaerephon by name, had asked the oracle at Delphi whether Socrates was the wisest of men; and the priestess there had responded affirmatively, although phrasing her answer in a significantly negative style. No man in Athens was wiser than Socrates, she said.

In his defense before the court Socrates described how this answer confused him. Though he did not underestimate his own knowledge, he knew of many men in Athens whose reputations for wisdom were much greater than his. He sensed that some "riddle," a mystery or symbolic teaching, was involved in the oracle's answer. "I know that I have no wisdom small or great," Socrates describes himself as having thought at the time. "What then can the god mean when he says that I am the wisest of men?"

"And yet," Socrates continued to think, "he is a god and cannot lie. That would be against his nature." There must be a riddle to it that needs to be deciphered. Nonetheless, he proceeded on the assumption that the god might indeed be wrong, and that he, Socrates, would prove the god to be wrong by finding a man in Athens who was wiser than he. Socrates then went about the town interviewing men of reputed eminence, to test their wisdom and report it to the god.

The results of his search were, however, not what he expected. Rather than refute the oracle, they indicated an answer to the riddle, and they made clear to Socrates the path of his vocation. When he interviewed the men of reputed wisdom in the community he found that they were full of doctrines and of intellectual opinions of various kinds, but that they were not really wise.

They felt that their knowledge of their special crafts, or their positions of responsibility in the community, gave them a superior knowledge of what Socrates calls "high matters," but that profundity of wisdom did not seem to be theirs. Indeed, their opinions about it and their conviction that they did possess wisdom were major obstacles to knowledge, although they did not recognize them as obstacles. Socrates at length concluded that since he was not filled with so many opinions, he was better off than they.

With this insight, he began to see through to the meaning of the riddle contained in the oracle's reply. Its meaning was not that Socrates was wise but that no man was wiser than he; and this was true simply because no man is wise of himself. Socrates' insight into the mystery was that that man alone is wise who realizes that his personal knowledge is worth nothing, and is not wisdom at all, no matter how much it may be inflated by social reputation or by self conceit.

Perceiving this, Socrates found a new dedication for his life. His task now was to go about among the community to raise questions that would arouse people and would cause them to examine their beliefs, to reconsider their opinions, until finally, recognizing that their doctrines are not wisdom, they would cast them aside as so much excess baggage. In his new role Socrates saw himself as one who goes about among men stirring them up to question themselves in order that they might recognize the flimsiness of their intellectual pretensions and eventually that they might discard their burden of false opinions so that they might travel light, in touch with the essence of truth.

It was in the course of this work that Socrates began to see himself in the image of a gadfly. He began to understand his role in life as comparable to that of an insect which goads or stings cattle, thus rousing them out of their lethargy and stimulating them to activity.

The comparison was deliberate. Human beings live as though in a sleep. Like cattle, they go through life automatically chewing their cud of superficial opinion never becoming aware of the superior food that lies latent within their capacities of knowledge, hidden and unused, but available to them. They have to be awakened from their unawareness and goaded to move onwards towards new recognitions of meaning in life.

Socrates' sense of vocation was that he felt himself to be the indispensable, although unpopular, goad working at the core of man. As the horse swipes at the gadfly with its tail, so would Socrates be an annoyance and be despised by other men.

He realized that his work would make him unpopular. Necessarily so, because the nature of the arousing he felt called to do required the raising of questions that would often have uncomfortable personal consequences. It would often involve a painful uprooting of accustomed habits of thinking, creating the painful condition of a psychological vacuum, at least temporarily when old conceptions are discarded before new ones have been reached. Sensing the painfulness of this vacuum to come, the person of conventional opinions tends to cling to his old viewpoint because of the security he feels in retaining the comfort of accustomed ways. It is an automatic response for the environmental self to slap the fly that awakens it. That old self would rather not become aware of the real self that is stirring within; and as long as it can slumber on, the encounter with reality will be avoided.

Socrates understood man's inherent reluctance to work toward truth, and he was therefore able to accept the opposition he would encounter in his calling. The effect of his goading would be, he knew, to upset the established pattern of life of those who, as he phrased it, "pretend to be something when they are really nothing."

In saying this, however, Socrates was not being contemptuous of his fellow man. He was referring simply to an inherent fact, a psychological fact, of man's life. Man's opinions of himself and his acceptance by others in the give and take of society result in feelings of self-importance that bloat his vanity with illusions. Ultimately man's pretending in the world is directed not so much towards others as towards himself, pretending that his outward accomplishments are "something" when they are "nothing." And yet the realization of the quality of truth involved in this "nothing" is the beginning of man's relationship to what is ultimately real in his life. It was toward this that Socrates' goading was directed.

From an operational point of view, Socrates' role as a gadfly called to goad man towards a living experience of truth was divided into two phases. In its first stage it was essentially a negative work. By the relentless goading of his questioning, Socrates was to lead men to the realization that their self-formed opinions are not made of the same stuff as wisdom is. Their conventional opinions are an illusory "nothing," a vanity separating them from reality. When these attitudes have been overcome, it becomes possible to touch those resources within the person that make a true "knowing" possible. That was the eventual goal of Socrates' goading.

The first stage of his work as gadfly was to neutralize the *impedimenta* of human opinion in order to clear the way for a fuller realization from within, by means, as Socrates put it, of "the divine faculty of which the internal oracle is the source." The second stage then involved a more affirmative style of goading, a drawing forth from the human person of those intimations of truth that inhere in his deepest nature. In this second, more constructive phase of his work, Socrates undertook to stir people not merely to question themselves and thus to neutralize their false opinions, but he sought to stir up and awaken the latent capacities of knowledge that rest unused, and often unsuspected, in the recesses of the individual mind.

A good instance of this affirmative style of goading is dramatized in the dialogue, "Meno." There, in a well-known passage, Socrates undertook to prove that a slave boy who had never been taught mathematics could have a knowledge of certain mathematical facts drawn forth from him by a skillful teacher. To do this, Socrates questioned the boy carefully, evoking from him by the processes of thought which he stirred in him, new insights of which the boy had not before been aware. From this Socrates deduced that teaching is not a matter of something being placed in one person by another, but is a question of eliciting something that is already present, although only implicitly and latently, at hidden depths of the individual's mind.

On the face of it, this demonstration accords very well with the style of modern thinking. The modern mind is quite prepared to understand what Socrates was doing and to agree with him in principle that the process of education at its best is a drawing forth of capacities of knowledge that are present but undeveloped in the individual. In the course of their being *led out* by the teacher a development takes place by which these capacities are fulfilled. That is the tone in which we would understand it in modern terms; but Socrates had quite another view of what was to be inferred from his demonstration with the untutored slave boy.

To him the facility with which he was able to draw new insights out of the boy was proof that the boy had known these things all along, but that he had not been aware of them. He had *forgotten* that he knew them. "Pay attention now," Socrates had said to Meno as he questioned the slave boy and directed the processes of his mind. "Observe whether he learns from me or whether he only remembers." It was clear that Socrates was not telling the boy what conclusions he should draw. He was not giving him the answers; he was only stimulating him to discover the answers himself by utilizing his own mental resources. This was what he spoke of as *remembering*.

"What we call learning," Socrates said by way of summary, "is only a process of recollection." This recollection, however, is not of events that have taken place in earlier years of the individual's life. At the outset of their interview Socrates had drawn a direct answer from the slave boy to the effect that at no time had he taken part in the study of mathematics. Meno, his master, who was Socrates' adversary in the argument, had verified this. The boy had not studied the subject, and yet he was able to demonstrate a significant insight into it. To us in modern times there are several different ways in which such an event can be understood; but to Socrates it was self-evident that the boy's capacity was the result of an experience he had had in a previous lifetime.

What has been called Socrates' "favorite doctrine" *
was at the base of this. It was a doctrine with a very ancient lineage, the belief that the immortality of the individual soul is expressed in many incarnations at different points in history. Socrates' special application of
it here was his view that the soul carries with it through
all its future incarnations the memories of its experiences, and of all the knowledge it has acquired in all
its earlier lives; but each time it is born into a new body
it forgets what it has known and is as ignorant then as
if it had never lived before.

The great task, then, as Socrates envisioned the problem of gaining knowledge, is to remember the things
that one has known in earlier lifetimes. It seems clear in
this connection that Socrates was interested primarily
not in recalling the personal events of previous exist-
ences, but in recalling the underlying capacities of
knowledge which had been accumulated in the course
of its past lives by the person (or specifically by his
"soul" as Socrates conceived of the soul).

He would not see much point, for example, in attempting to identify the names and places of persons
in whose form an individual had lived during previous
incarnations; neither did he care to remember daily
events, nor to recall emotional, personal encounters.
These would have a subjectivity and pettiness that
would place them beyond the pale of his primary con-

* See Cebes speaking in the *Phaedo.*

cerns. He would be interested, however, in establishing a connection and new relationship with the qualities of cognition which had been developed in past
experiences, such as one's relationship with mathematics,
or with medicine, or with poetry.

Such qualities of experience, representing underlying
capacities of knowledge, would be of great relevance
because they would provide access to larger awareness
for the person in his present life. It would be necessary,
however, that a special sensitivity to this level of the
soul be established; and Socrates saw himself as the
gadfly who acted to *evoke* this sensitivity among his
fellow Athenians. This was the spirit in which he said
encouragingly to Meno to stimulate him in this interest, "Be of good cheer, and try to recollect what you do
not know, or rather what you do not remember."

In this we can see the specific goal that Socrates set
forth for the second stage of his calling as a gadfly
among men. In the first phase of it, he used a methodology of reasoning to stir men up to recognize the lim-
itedness of their established opinions. He wanted to
neutralize the vanities of which their view of life was
formed, and he undertook to achieve this by a close
questioning as to what they really believed.

The intention behind this questioning was to reach
a point where the previously accepted beliefs would
no longer be felt to be convincing in terms of intellect,
and the person would then be forced back into himself

to pay attention to the "internal oracle," the voice of essential wisdom within. His consciousness would be turned away from environmental vanities to the realm of remembrances within, where knowledge that is present but not accessible could be recalled and made available for use.

Socrates' goal as a goad was to stir men up so that the traces of knowledge garnered through the timeless journey of the soul could come alive again. He sought to open a way for the true wisdom of which the oracle had spoken. His goal was to touch the depths in men, to evoke what was hidden and unremembered there, in order that it might serve as an inward source of truth.

We can see at this point a striking similarity between the calling of Socrates and the trend of work emerging in modern depth psychology. Both proceed on the hypothesis that the resources of wisdom are hidden in the depths of the human being, and that they are best able to unfold in meaning when they are stirred to full expression.

Where Socrates' way was a *goading*, the corresponding psychological way is *evoking*. In Socratic terms, the process of stirring the depths involves a calling up of remembrances of knowledge gained through the fullness of time in a range of experience that reaches far beyond an individual lifetime. In the terms of depth psychology, the process of *psyche-evoking* is a rousing to activity of potentials that are inherent in the organic depths of the person, by which intimations of meaning are drawn forth out of the dark core of the psycho-physical unity of being. This is a relatively new way in psychology, and it derives from a recognition of the fact that procedures based on analytical reductionism are fit for describing pathology and for alleviating it, but that they stymie the creative processes of the psyche. The point of view of psycho*analysis* is therefore giving way, and is being supplanted by conceptions that reflect the dynamics of psyche-*evoking*. We shall see more of the details of this as our discussion proceeds.

One important difference is to be noted between the Socratic way and the psychological way. The one speaks in the terms of traditional philosophy, drawing upon images that reach far into the past of classical mythology. The other phrases its insights in the style of modern science and seeks to establish its relation to the timeless images of life in terms that meet the criteria of modern knowledge. This is indeed an important difference, but it is a connection as well. Both modern psychology and the Socratic way are instances of man's disciplined attempts to reach toward reality in modes of thought that fit the tone and temper of their times. Beyond their differences in style lies a quality of integrity that unites them; and from this unity we may eventually be able to draw the model of a psychological and spiritual perspective that will answer our modern need.

TWO PERSPECTIVES IN DEPTH PSYCHOLOGY: PATHOLOGY AND POTENTIALITY

Its similarity to the mission of Socrates tells us a great deal about the nature and role of depth psychology in our time. It has been called into being to meet an urgent need of modern man, to provide a *way* by which the modern person can achieve a larger experience of meaning in his existence. A psychological awakening of spiritual force is involved in this, the stirring of presently unused potentials of awareness. To evoke this in modern man is the goal of the new psychology, as it was for Socrates among the ancient Athenians.

We must realize, however, that it was not at all with thoughts like these that depth psychology began in Europe about a century ago. At that time, as a by-product of the tremendous technological and cultural changes taking place, changes that involved large-scale migrations from rural areas to cities, the rapid rise of machine industry on a mass production basis, the extension of personal freedom, and the broadening of education to large classes of persons, especially to women for the first time, the traditional styles of behavior broke apart. People who, in an earlier generation would have followed the traditional patterns of life, participating in prearranged marriages, conventional religious observances, and remaining close to the family unit all their lives, now found themselves adrift. Often they were geographically at a distance from the groups they would otherwise have depended upon for their emotional supports. Separated and alone, they had to chart the course of their lives by themselves with a minimum of traditions to guide them. They found themselves under the pressure of having to make many difficult personal decisions in an increasingly competitive society.

Some made these decisions well, or at least successfully from an economic and cultural point of view, and took their place in the prosperity of the new European economy. Others could not meet the pace of the changes. They became confused, and fell by the wayside, not knowing how to adjust their lives to the new, more flexible canons of morality.

Their confusion expressed itself in breakdowns of personality on all levels. These were psychological breakdowns with all the bizarre symptoms that psychological illness entails; and there were also physical illnesses of many kinds, derived ultimately from the personal disharmonies resulting from the changes in Western culture. It was not, however, until the twentieth century that definitive advances were made in demonstrating that many apparently physical illnesses have a psychological, and ultimately social, root.

When these new varieties of illnesses occurred in the new technological culture of Europe, the person to whom they were taken for healing was the medical doctor. It was natural that this should be so, since the symptoms were experienced as disease. In addition, there was no other profession in the community to whom people could go with this kind of problem, unless they went to the minister; but for a great many of these troubled people, their problems had arisen precisely because traditional religion no longer spoke to their pressing needs. Unfortunately, people could seldom recognize at the time that it was doubts about personal morality and about larger questions of the meaning of life that were the sources of their difficulties. The outer manifestations of their problems seemed much too objective to have subjective roots. Therefore they turned to the medical doctor for a cure; and he conscientiously sought to effect a healing by referring to the physiological and neurological terms which he knew best and to which he was accustomed.

It came about in this general way that the illnesses resulting from the breakdown of the traditional beliefs about the conduct and meaning of life were taken to the medical doctor for treatment. He interpreted them, according to the habits of thinking in which he had been trained, in the light of pathology. He studied the symptoms, sought out the "causes," and diligently attempted to devise methods of treatment. This was the spirit in which Sigmund Freud carried out his work in the late nineteenth century, on the basis of which he developed an integrated theory of the functioning of the psyche. It should be noted, however, that this was a description of the psychic processes studied specifically from the point of view of the genesis of pathologic conditions.

The system of *psychoanalysis*, which was the product of Freud's studies, was thus developed within the framework of medical thinking, and it retained the characteristic medical preconceptions about the relation of pathology to treatment. It has continued to conceive itself and to be thought of by others as a branch of medicine, but the experience and observations of many psychoanalysts has been pointing in the opposite direction. Psychological practice has led to increasing recognition of the fact that a perspective much larger than pathology is necessary if one is to develop a healthy and constructive psyche.

The problem may be stated simply in this way. When a person contracts an illness like measles or chicken pox, the disease is a well definable entity. It has certain specific symptoms by which it may be recognized, and these are connected to definite "causes" which may be treated or may be permitted to run their course, a predictable course, until the illness disappears. The disease will then have come and gone within the person, and it will have displayed an individuality of its own. It will have behaved as an entity, following a certain pattern of principles for its coming and going.

In contrast to this, experience has shown increasingly that psychological illnesses do not behave like entities. They do not enter the life of the person and then leave. They rather *are* the life of the person. They are even the destiny, or the channel by which an important aspect of the specific meaning of the individual's life unfolds. This is particularly true of sensitive persons who eventually find an important work for their lives, or who achieve an especially intense spiritual awareness. The culminating experience by which new capacities of awareness open to such persons to give new content and meaning to the activities of their lives, often looks deceptively like illness while it is still in its early stages. If it would be diagnosed and treated in the light of pathology at that point in its genesis, all the possibilities of development would be cut short before they had a chance to grow. This point has been well interpreted in the writings of Otto Rank* and in the works of William James before him.†

We are brought thus to a question of orientation, a question of the attitude with which we shall approach the individual human being. When a person shows signs of internal stress, shall we interpret this stress in terms of the symptomology of illness or shall we look into it to find the seeds of growth? And shall we then, rather than diagnose a particular syndrome as though it were a fixed entity in the individual, seek a means of drawing forth the potentials of the person?

This is much more than a question of personal philosophy or of subjective attitude. It involves, quite objectively, the possibilities of development in the person

* See Ch. VII in my earlier book, *The Death and Rebirth of Psychology*.
† See especially his masterpiece, which is a great precursor of modern depth psychology, *The Varieties of Religious Experience*.

and therefore the possibilities of health as well as creativity.

We find that the process of personal growth includes several stages in which the individual exhibits symptoms of marked personality disturbance. There may be the situation, for example, in which the person experiences a serious doubt as to whether he will be able to fulfill the image of achievement he has set for himself. In the nature of things, such an image comes ahead of the fact of achievement, and there is an interim period during which the outcome is in doubt. At such a time a major crisis may develop in which the meaning of life as a whole is called into question so that there will even be mention of suicide. Many a young artist or poet, or budding physician or minister goes through a period like this. Shall it be diagnosed in terms of its symptoms and treated as an instance of pathology to be eliminated as an entity of disease? Or shall it be treated as an inherent aspect and necessary stage in the process of personal growth as a whole?

If the latter be the case, there are specific psychological techniques one can follow to enter into the process by which growth is trying to come through and in which it is being stymied. One can enter the process to reach into the depth of the psyche to where the seed of potentiality is pressing toward growth. One can touch that seed there to evoke its strength and to generate a momentum that will enable the person to move forward to the next stage of development, and eventually to the further stage of conflict that must inevitably follow in the cycles of growth.

The important point in carrying this through successfully is to refrain deliberately from premature diagnosis. When symptoms of disturbance appear where these symptoms are part of the process of personal growth, the meaning and potentiality of development is missed if it is interpreted in the light of pathology.

When the person becomes self-consciously analytical, the momentum of growth is lost. This is so for several reasons, any one of which can permanently stunt the process of creative development. One reason is that when the person begins to think of himself in the light of pathology his image grows dim. The thoughts he projects are thoughts of weakness and they refer to the difficulties experienced along the road of development rather than to the unfolding essence of the process as a whole. When they are described and diagnosed and are given the respectability of pathologic forms, they become entities with a reality of their own. The focus of attention is then placed upon the transient pathology of the process and the energy latent in the seed of potentiality is not drawn upon. One of the primary principles in constructive psychological work is to replace diagnostic analysis by a method of evoking from the depths of the psyche the energy latent in the seed of potentiality.

In achieving this, it is most important to develop an inward perspective of the process that includes the purpose implicit in it as well as a feeling for the rhythms by which it is emerging. This sense of inward time, involving as it does a recognition of the reality of the elusive process unfolding within the personality, enables an individual to keep his bearings during the risings and the fallings, the disturbances and doubts of which the process is composed. It is this awareness that finally makes it possible for the energy contained in the seed-image to come to expression in activities of life so that a momentum of growth can establish itself. With this, the symptoms of pathology are overcome and are replaced by images and behavior of greater strength and fruitfulness.

From the point of view of the depth psychologist, the primary goal in practice is to establish in the person with whom he is working a sensitivity to the inward process of the psyche. This is the very opposite of a self-conscious analytical diagnosis of oneself. It is a feeling of movement, a feeling of a master cycle of life, which proceeds within the person and includes tensions and rhythms, doubts and dynamics of many kinds. It involves a sense of inner time, an inward perspective. To achieve this requires some continuity of personal psychological work in order to develop an intuitive sense and familiarity with what is taking place at the depth of the psyche, and above all, to develop a sensitivity to the symbolic style in which the movements in the psyche are expressed.

While this sensitivity to the inward process is being

developed, a particular attitude is called for on the part of the depth psychologist himself. This is an attitude of connection to the seed of the other person, an acceptance of it without defining it (so as not to limit its potentiality by his own preconceptions), and a sensitive openness to the process by which it is unfolding. In a profound sense this is an attitude of love, for it involves an affirmation of the seed of potentiality in the other person *even while that seed has not disclosed its specific form.*

On the surface of the personality one will see the disturbances and conflicts which could easily be misanalyzed as the symptoms of pathology. It is necessary to feel beyond these to what is present but latent in the depths of the person. It is necessary to reach through to what is there but has not yet disclosed itself. The depth psychologist must be able to feel through to reach and affirm that seed of meaningful life in the other person even while it has not yet made itself visible. This is why it is basically an attitude of love.

Among its many aspects, love is an affirmation of that which is felt as real but cannot be seen. When the tulip has grown, one can admire its beauty; but that admiration is not love. He who feels the beauty of the tulip while it is still in the bulb covered by snow has love for the tulip. So also does one human being have love for his fellow man when he affirms the seed of potentiality in him even while it is covered over by the snows of emotional disturbance and stress. By love he affirms the seed and evokes the flow of symbolic material which will enable it to unfold. He deliberately does not turn the process of growth back upon itself by analysis that diagnoses special phases without reference to the whole. To do this would miss the flow of wholeness implicit in the depths of personality. It would miss the opportunity to evoke the creative element which is the core of health in the human spirit.

Considering these things, we realize that there are two distinct aspects to modern depth psychology. One is its role as a therapy for emotional illness. This is related to psychopathology and has primarily a medical tone. It is this quality of work in which depth psychology had its origins.

The second aspect of depth psychology is emergent, emergent in a double sense. Firstly, because the quality of spiritual concern that has emerged in depth psychology during the past generation could hardly have been anticipated from the emphasis on diagnostic analysis with which it originated. And secondly, because its work now is increasingly directed toward drawing forth an emergent quality in man, an integral awareness of being, out of the mire of tension and emotional confusion.

In its second aspect, depth psychology becomes the discipline that works toward the development of the personality as a whole. Its primary goal is no longer therapy as such. It no longer concentrates on removing specific symptoms of so-called mental illness. Its goal now is to draw forth the fullness of the potential of the person; and in the course of this, therapy does take place. It takes place naturally and in a perspective of growth, not merely removing old symptoms but opening new avenues of meaning. Therapy becomes then not a deliberate and conscious goal in the new psychology, but an incidental and yet inevitable by-product of the emergent experience of wholeness at the core of personality.

This indirect approach to healing follows naturally from the basic insight into the relation between psychopathology and the vacuum of meaning in modern experience. The evidence of psychotherapy is accumulating to show that what has been called pathology is indeed not a fact in itself, but a derivative of the emptiness of personality. Lacking an integrative experience to give cohesion to life, the individual splinters into segments; and this condition of segmentation is what gives the pain and confusion of neurosis. To paste the parts together may alleviate the pain and even give the impression that the person has been "fixed" and that the pathology of brokenness has been healed; but this is an illusion. Pasting will not last, for the lines of weakness remain. Only a unifying experience that establishes anew a sense of wholeness as a principle working within the person can have a lastingly healing effect.

An experience of this kind involves a unifying contact within oneself; and also, through oneself, an intimation of reality beyond. Here the sense of wholeness becomes more than psychological; and we find, perhaps paradoxically, that when the level of experience moves beyond psychology, psychological effects of tremendous impact become possible.

A minimum of what happens then is that the new awareness of reality that has been felt both within and around oneself eliminates those pains and disorders that had been diagnosed as pathology. It achieves this primarily by placing them in a new perspective in which they can naturally, without self-consciousness, play a meaningful and constructive role. The maximum of what happens is that the seed of life is touched in the person and begins to grow again. This, which is the largest success for which one can hope, is the simplest of psychological effects. It is elemental. It restores the natural functioning of the processes that are inherent in the psyche, so that the person can become what it is his nature to be. In this context, depth psychology is the art of doing for the psyche what the psyche would do for itself if it could, understanding that the goal inherent in the psyche is that it enable the patterns of potentiality within it to unfold in life.* When this is achieved the

---

* I am paraphrasing here Dr. Herbert Ratner's definition of medicine "as the art of doing for nature what nature would do for herself if she could." See the pamphlet entitled, "Medicine, an interview by Dwight McDonald with Herbert Ratner, M.D.," published in the American Character Series, Center for the Study of Democratic Institutions, The Fund for the Republic, Santa Barbara, Calif., 1962. Dr. Ratner's statement is a brilliant critique of the medical attitudes permeating our "overmedicated" society. He presents, too, a wise reminder of the sense of wholeness in man that underlies the medical philosophy of Hippocrates.

healing of pathology becomes inevitable, because an intimation of wholeness has been experienced in a symbolic form at the core of the person. And such intimations, as we shall presently see when we turn to study individual life experiences, provide sufficient vision to give meaning for a lifetime.

3 Psyche: The principle of direction and the place of depth

In the history of depth psychology, the key term has been *the unconscious*. The main progress in the field has been made with this as the prime hypothesis. It is significant to observe, therefore, that there are several reasons to believe that the phrase, *the unconscious*, will probably not long remain in use. The connotations as well as the content of the term are too negative and restrictive to serve as an adequate vehicle for the emergent conception of growth. The psychological use of the term derives primarily from the period in the development of depth psychology when the pathology of personality was emphasized. Now, as depth psychology continues to enlarge the scope of its studies, and especially as it carries the hypothesis of unfolding potentiality in man into fields of religion, art, and the history of culture, it requires a large unitary term capable of conveying the key conception of integrative wholeness as the operative principle in man.

The use of the term, *the unconscious*, which seems to be the weakest and may be expected to pass out of usage the soonest, places emphasis upon *"the."* Speaking of *the* unconscious, presents the term as a noun and carries the implication that the unconscious is a fixed entity. We can agree with its use as an adjective to describe a quality of cognition, but it is not accurate to refer to it as though it were an organ of the human being. It is an aspect of knowing, a form of cognition, or of non-cognition as the case may be; but it is not comparable to an arm or a leg. Nonetheless, it is often spoken of in the older literature of depth psychology as though it were. The quality of personality that is involved here has a most elusive quality. It will not permit itself to be trapped and held and encompassed in a phrase. Even to find a term that will describe it aptly is exceedingly difficult; but it is necessary, at least, to avoid misleading implications. Especially because the conception that is involved here lies at the heart of the new directions of depth psychology, we require a terminology that will provide a wide latitude and flexibility in exploring the depths of personality.

To speak of *the unconscious* does, however, serve a useful function. It does communicate the involuntary style of knowledge and the inadvertent expressions that characterize human behavior, especially where emotion and the reaching toward an experience of meaning in life is concerned.

The term, the unconscious, has been used to refer to the area of the personality where two general types of mental contents are found. One is the repressed material of individual experience; the other is the generic or universal images which provide the bases for experiences in art and in religion.

The use of the term as Sigmund Freud developed it was directed primarily toward describing the results of experiences which the individual cannot bear to retain in his conscious mind. He therefore represses them into his "unconscious." This referred to the memory of events that were painful; or the wish for experiences that were not socially approved. Not permitting himself to dwell upon these wishes or memories, the individual would, without realizing it, press them out of his conscious mind, thinking he would then be rid of them. The great discovery of Freud, which was the starting point for modern depth psychology, was his realization that when thoughts are repressed, they are not destroyed but continue in another form in which they have even greater consequences. They work on at a hidden level of the personality, in the unconscious, specifically in the part of it that Freud called the "unconscious repressed." When C. G. Jung undertook to interpret this aspect of experience in a larger context of thought, he called this area of repressed individual material, the *personal unconscious.**

The material of the repressed, or personal, unconscious is, however, only one aspect of the depth of personality. In his first pioneering book, "The Interpretation of Dreams," Freud saw the importance of understanding those factors in the personality that are more fundamental than the mechanisms of repression. Jung was impressed by this conception, and he made it a starting point for a far-reaching inquiry. His goal was to mark off and define the patterns of development that are at the core of personality, underlying what he called the "personal unconscious."

The result of these researches on one level was the conception of archetypes. This referred to the tendencies of behavior that are universal, or are at least generic, to the nature of man. It is a theory that opens many avenues of study, but of even broader implications is the conception of the unconscious to which it leads. It suggests that the foundations of behavior, which the theory of the unconscious was seeking to in-

* For a full discussion of the historical development of the theory of the unconscious from Freud to Jung, see Progoff, *The Death and Rebirth of Psychology*, New York, Julian Press, 1956, Chaps. IV, V, and VI.

terpret, are to be understood not in terms of repressions but in terms of patterns of development that are inherent in the human organism. In these terms, the primary quality of the unconscious would have to be seen as a growth or unfoldment of patterns of potentiality. Its tone would express not the backward movement of repression but the forward movement of a development by which the nature of the individual fulfills itself. Following this line of thought, one could see that the unconscious is actually that part of the human being that contains those potentialities, which, if they are brought to expression, carry out the purpose of life in the person.

The style by which the unconscious functions is thus primarily not repressive but purposive. The question to ask of it is not: what is it hiding? But: what is it trying to unfold? This realization was the basis of the shift in emphasis that marked the controversy between Freud and the psychoanalysts on the one hand and the proponents of Alfred Adler and C. G. Jung on the other. Adler and Jung perceived that the characteristic of what had been spoken of as the unconscious was purposive development in the midst of, and in response to, the difficulties of life. Each in his way then proceeded to work out a full theoretical system on the basis of this awareness; and in doing so they opened new vistas for depth psychology.

As a result of their work, we have come to a point where we can see that a much more affirmative formulation is required to describe the area of personality that has been studied under the term, *the unconscious*. A more appropriate name seems now to be called for, a name that will include the quality of consciousness and inner guidance that is implicit in the nonconscious processes of human personality.

As a matter of usage a new term does seem to be emerging to replace *the unconscious*. It is *psyche*. Sometimes it appears with an adjective making it more specific. Occasionally, especially in the writings of his later years, Jung used the phrase, the Objective Psyche, in order to emphasize the constructive aspects of what he had very misleadingly named, the *Collective Unconscious*.* He wanted to correct certain misconceptions to which his older term had led. In another context, developing the concepts of depth psychology in the perspective of modern biology, I used the term, *Organic Psyche*, to emphasize the close relationship between the psyche and natural evolution. This conception tends rather to draw together the thought of Alfred Adler and that of Jung with respect to the nonconscious, purposive process of personality.†

It seems, upon reconsideration, that adjectives added to the term *psyche* are not especially helpful. What is

* See, in this connection, Progoff, *Jung's Psychology and Its Social Meaning* (Julian Press and Evergreen Reprint). Chap. II, "The Psyche and the Layers of Consciousness," deals with the problem of the unconscious within the framework of Jung's thought. See also, Michael Fordham, *The Objective Psyche*, London, Routledge, 1961.

† See Progoff, *Depth Psychology and Modern Man*, New York, Julian Press, 1959, Chap. VI, "The Urge toward Ongoing Life," and Chap. VII,"The Organic Psyche and Its Contents."

important is that we understand what the psyche is in its essentials. Especially if we can get a good *feeling* comprehension of its elements and of the principles behind its processes, the details of its functioning will disclose themselves to us later.

In its essence, the psyche is the directive principle in the human being which guides its growth from the moment of conception forward. As the embryo of a human being is formed, certain tendencies of growth are set; and if nothing untoward happens such as severe illness or accident, these tendencies will fulfill themselves through the life-cycle of the individual. The embryo will become an infant, it will grow as a child, its body and mental capacities will mature according to a general pattern of stages until maturity is reached. All of this will follow a directing principle that is inherent in the seed of the individual organism and begins to unfold from the moment that the seed of it is fully formed and begins to grow. The process of unfoldment then moves forward, interacting with the environment, persisting under the impulse of the underlying urge to life, in the direction of the possibilities of growth that were present in the seed at the moment of inception. The principle that guides the process of growth all through the life of the individual is what we speak of as *psyche*. Psyche is the directing principle in the individual that sets the pattern of growth and works to sustain it throughout the life of the organism.

In this sense the psyche is a unitary principle in human life. It is not conscious as opposed to unconscious; neither is it unconscious as opposed to conscious. It is both together. The tendencies of development are not determined by the individual, but arise spontaneously out of his organic nature. At the same time they express and are directed by a quality of knowing that is intelligent even though its actions are not consciously decided upon. The inherent processes of growth take place with awareness and with a set, though variable, direction *as though* they were consciously guided toward a specific purpose. It is this *as though-ness* that is the essence of the psyche. This is the quality that leads to many of the paradoxes of human existence. The task of depth psychology is to enter into the psyche in such a way that it touches both its unknowing and its wisdom, linking consciousness and what has been called the unconscious in an integral unity that achieves a fuller development of personality.

The psyche in a human being carries the unfolding purpose of his life, but in a form that is difficult to trace. The psyche is elusive because it is intangible, but it is the thread of unity in the individual's existence nonetheless. Outwardly it discloses itself in the pattern of events that comprise a person's biography, his works in the world, his social relationships. Inwardly the psyche is composed of something that is much more difficult to recognize. It is made up of inward events, dreams, images, tensions, fears, desires, intuitions. These are difficult to grasp, and difficult to define; but it is these that are the effective and formative factors in the psyche.

Dreams are particularly useful for giving us insight into the forces that are working within the person. They indicate the quality of what is being formed in the depth of the psyche before it is embodied in events in the outer world. In a similar way, artworks such as poems and paintings and novels give us tangible evidence of what is taking place within an individual. The content of these is not consciously created; they express the unconscious aspect of the psyche. When these are observed as they appear, one after another in the order in which they come forth from the psyche, the dreams, images, artworks, and acts in the world form a continuity in which a pattern of development becomes visible. Gradually one is able to perceive in perspective the rhythms and cycles by which the personality grows, suffers, and grows again. A unity of being emerges in which the outer embodiments of the individual's life are seen as integrally connected to the images of potentiality and fear expressed in the symbolism of the inner life. Over a period of time, the form of a whole person takes shape, inward and outer, and one can recognize the distinct style, the tone, and rhythm by which the psyche of this unique human being, each unique human being, is unfolding and fulfilling itself. This thread of unity, moving forward and forming itself in the continuity of personal life, revealing itself in its inward coherence and in its outward embodiments, is the essence of the psyche

MOVEMENT AND SYMBOLIC STYLE

By what means does the psyche of an individual manifest itself in life? It does this by action that embodies in the world a potentiality that was indicated in advance as an image, in the form of a dream, or as a waking vision. It begins on the level of intuition as a nonconscious intimation of things to come.

Here we have the key to the pattern by which personality develops. The process of growth begins with an image of its goal, though this image does not consciously direct itself. It simply appears. Even when it is not in the visual form of a specific image, it is present; and it expresses itself then as a nonconscious knowing of what is true *in principle*. It is present as an image of the new condition which the psyche is engaged in bringing to actuality. It is a goal that is an active factor in the person because it is a potentiality working to fulfill itself. Neither the goal nor the manner of its fulfillment are thought out in advance; nor are they rationally decided upon. The entire pattern discloses itself as it acts itself out; and often it is only in the course of this enactment that the person discovers the nature of the goal he is truly seeking.

The image is a representation of the purpose that is implicit in the urge to embark upon a particular course of action. In general terms, it is comparable to the way a bird builds its nest without consciously knowing what the final purpose of its act is to be. It is drawn onward and it goes ahead. Similarly a human being often finds himself drawn irresistibly onto a course of action without knowing in advance what its ultimate outcome will be.

Many instances of this come to mind in the lives of creative persons. One thinks, for example, of Herman Melville as a young man going to sea on a whaling ship with no possible way of knowing that the seeds were being planted for one of the world's great expeditions into the dimension of symbols. The writing of his novel, *Moby Dick*, lay completely in the future, but something drew him forward towards it. His experience at that time, as throughout the later creative years of his life, was as though one of his legs stepped forward on its own without his deciding it, and the other leg was forced to follow and step a little further. Thus he was drawn on towards attainments without limit, never knowing the ending nor even the immediate goal. He did not decide it, and yet something within him forced it to be. He wrote of this in his letters to Nathaniel Hawthorne, and the tone of their correspondence implies that they both recognized such a factor in their lives.*

In personal psychological work we can see with especial clarity how it is that images come ahead of actions

* I am indebted for my information on the process of growth in Herman Melville to a work-in-progress on this subject by Daniel C. Noel.

to set the pattern and direction for them. The process of personal growth often begins, at least symbolically, with an image that previsions the eventual achievement; and as the process moves forward, the various phases of frustration and progress are further represented in imagery form.

I think in this connection of a young woman, whose writing ability was pushing itself to the fore. She found that her creative life was symbolized in her dreams by a certain opera star. It was, for various personal reasons, Madame Tebaldi, for she typified to the dreamer the modern woman who succeeds in creative work. The image appeared first as an expression of the total possibility of development, the goal toward which the entire process of growth was tending. The process of growth, however, does not move in a straight line upward. The personality does not go directly to its final achievement by the shortest route. Much circling and indirection, much blockage and apparent stymying of the process is inherent in it. Thus, at one stage of our work, the image of the opera star appeared in a dream as a deformed woman trying to sing; and later she appeared as a woman singing without an audience. These expressed the various difficulties which the image was encountering in attempting to fulfill itself. As the work continued, the image appeared in other forms and eventually arrived at the point where its creative power could be lived out in the life of the young woman as a writer.

It appears, and we shall be in a better position to understand this in the course of the chapters that follow, that the unfoldment of an image has a certain life-cycle peculiar to itself. It goes through a period, or several periods, of attrition, which lead eventually to experiences of larger and more meaningful contact with life. The rhythms of this vary with each individual, but if one stays with the underlying process of the psyche, if one stays true to it, a balancing and fulfillment occurs which brings a realization of wholeness as an active fact in life. If the individual remains authentically committed to the process of growth in the psyche, the image eventually bears its flower.

When this finally comes to pass, the individual who experiences it becomes aware of a pattern of meaning in his life. He realizes that there is a direction of development unfolding in his personal existence, and that he did not put it there. It is part of him, but it is not his creation. It is disclosing itself to him while it expresses itself within him. He is then in the position of having to turn his attention to this principle to learn from it the purpose unfolding in the background of his life.

The experience of this is personal, but it has overtones of larger significance. Since the purpose emerging in the individual is not of his own making, there is the implication that its source is elsewhere, that the purpose unfolding in his individual life is in some way connected to a larger purpose of life unfolding transpersonally in the universe. The perception of this, and the feeling that accompanies it, is subjective; but the basis of the experience itself is objective. It derives from the nature of the psyche itself.

The essence of the psyche is that it is the directive principle by means of which meaning unfolds in the individual's existence. It is a principle that operates not only in human beings but in sub-human species as well. The tendency is observed throughout the natural world that individual beings are drawn in a direction that fulfills the potentialities of their nature. The psyche is the faculty by means of which this occurs. When the principle of meaning, which the psyche embodies, is experienced intensely by an individual, it has the effect of opening in him a sensitivity to meaningfulness not only in his personal life but in the universe around him. He feels connected to a purpose that expresses itself through him in his personal existence and that also encompasses him in a way that he can feel but can define only with difficulty.

This quality of awareness expresses man's need to experience the meeting of the finite and the infinite within himself. The psyche seems to be the one faculty in man capable of serving as the bridge and making this meeting possible. This is so because in functioning as the directive principle in man it brings about an experience of purpose in individual existence. The awareness of purpose and the recognition of it in the life process has the effect of transcending individuality. In recognizing a purpose unfolding within his individual existence, the person cannot avoid intimations of a larger purpose as well in which the meaning of his individual existence is encompassed and included.

By its very nature, therefore, the functioning of the psyche tends to have a connective effect. As it brings about an experience of meaning within the person, it awakens in the finite being a sensitivity to the infinite. It leads to the realization that since this sensitivity is possible it must be that somewhere in the depths of the finite person there lies a capacity to perceive some of the meanings implicit in the infinite.

This capacity is indeed a primary aspect of the psyche. It is closely connected to the fact that the psyche is the directive principle by which purpose emerges in the life of man. It is the means by which the individual participates in the meaningful unfoldment of infinity and thus uncovers meaning in his own existence. A major quality of the psyche is its sensitivity to the large patterns of meaning in the universe. It *reflects* these in man. The psyche is a mirror of the patterns of meaning that give form to the infinite. Naturally the reflection is not the reality, but it does indicate that the reality is actually there.

The reflections of reality in the mirror of the psyche are necessarily imperfect versions of the original. This is so for several reasons, but primarily it is because they are representations of the infinite in finite form. The fullness of the infinite cannot be contained in the human perception of it. It is as though one tried to carry a quart of milk in a half-pint jar. Much would overflow and be lost, but enough would remain to give the taste of the milk. This is how man receives his intimations of larger dimensions of reality. Of the abundance that is available, a small part comes within the range of his awareness; and this is further limited by the cultural patterns and prejudices that restrict human cognition. Incomplete though it is, enough is perceived to give man a strong intimation of the quality of reality that is reflected in his psyche.

These intimations of larger truths are mirrored in the psyche and are perceived as images. The form of these images may be visual, coming as pictures; they may be auditory, coming as words, or sounds, or music; they may be olfactory, coming as smells that carry the scent of what is sought; and very often these images express themselves, strongly but elusively, in the more generalized terms of intuitive feeling.

Whatever the form in which they appear, the primary quality of the images is that they are symbolic. To say that the imagery of the psyche is symbolic means that it is indirect and allusive. It does not state its meanings in specific, logical terms, but it *portrays* its meanings. For example, when movement is to be conveyed, the idea of motion is not stated but an object in motion is depicted, perhaps a train, or an automobile, or airplane. When a particular emotion is felt, the imagery of the psyche does not state that emotion explicitly but it establishes an atmosphere through which the emotion is conveyed.

Usually this atmosphere is created by the tone of a story or a sequence of events that is presented on the level of imagery. That is the nature of dreams. In the dream it is as though a small scenario is acted out. There is action and a plot, and a theme that gives the dream cohesion. This theme, whatever it may be in the individual case, is the essence of the dream and the point toward which the dream is moving; but it is symbolic. This means that it makes its point by dramatization and by atmosphere rather than by direct statement.

A brief example may enable us to observe these traits of symbolism concretely. These are the traits of all dreams that are more than just rehearsals or replays of outer events; that is, every dream that expresses the inward concerns and development of the individual in any aspect proceeds in a symbolic style.

As an instance, let us follow this dream of Emma, a woman who was on the verge of losing hope for herself when the dream appeared. In the dream Emma was in a taxi and she was headed for an airport. She knew in the dream that she had to be on time to board a plane that was scheduled to depart at nine o'clock. There seemed to be plenty of time, but the taxi was caught in one traffic jam after another. In front of it, other cars were in accidents or had breakdowns; the taxi would move and then would come to a red light and have to wait. At one point, a boat had to pass under a drawbridge and all the cars had to wait. It was one delay after another for which the taxi driver himself was not to blame. Though the trip had started in plenty of time to make the plane, now Emma felt in the dream that it was getting dangerously late. As the taxi was nearing the vicinity of the airport with several minutes of driving time still remaining, she leaned forward and asked the driver what time it was. He looked at his watch and said to her, "Two minutes to nine." They both realized then that they would not arrive at the airport in time for the nine o'clock departure.

At that point in the dream, Emma experienced a moment of intense consciousness. She felt that she had a major decision to make, and it seemed to be a momentous decision that depended totally upon her judgment. Should she tell the driver to turn the taxi around and take her home, since she had apparently missed her plane? Her habitual style of behavior inclined her to this. Or should she continue to drive on to the airport anyway, even though there seemed to be no point in going on? Not knowing why, she decided on the latter course. The ride continued, and soon they reached the gate at the entrance to the airport. The taxi stopped and Emma explained her problem to the sentry on duty. He replied that the plane she was to have boarded was leaving at that very moment, but perhaps it was still on the field. He would phone ahead to the takeoff area and find out. Sure enough, she was in luck. The propellers were turning but the plane was still on the field, and the captain of the plane was willing to wait for her if she would hurry right down. Yes, certainly she would hurry; and she awakened from the dream.

There was a definite message in this dream, a message that came through to Emma with great strength. The dream, she felt, was recapitulating the situations of her life in outline. Getting off to a good start, she had run into one unavoidable delay after another, until finally it seemed that her opportunities were gone. She had always felt that she had an appointment with destiny, that something of significance would happen in her life; but now it seemed that, inexplicably, she had missed her chance. Somehow, suddenly it seemed to be too late. That was the situation in which she found herself living at the time of the dream. The decision which was required of her in the dream corresponded to a life-decision, a fundamental, existential decision which she was then in process of making. Should she give up and accept the mishaps of her life as indications that her life was a failure with no meaning and no fruit? Or should she go ahead with her life on the slim hope that some unpredictable good fortune might still be hers?

On the conscious level Emma favored the former course. Her rational judgment inclined her to believe that there was no reason for her to continue to hope. But when she came to see me to tell me the dream, her decision to go ahead and say yes to life was already made. She felt that the dream had made the decision for her, and that under such circumstances she had no alternative but to follow its guidance. In fact, Emma drew from the dream a feeling of special support and validity. Its message brought a new sense of personal affirmation to her life, a realization that a source of guidance and meaning was present within her very nature. With this, a new interest in existence awakened in her.

In the short run perspective, the dream had a revitalizing effect upon her. For the long run, it opened access to an inward source that sustained her during the difficult period that followed. Now that she had come to the new conclusion that it would be worthwhile for her to live after all, the day-to-day task of rebuilding her life lay ahead of her.

Emma's dream, considered as a unity, is a good illustration of what is meant by speaking of the *symbolic* style of the psyche. The dream was carrying a definite message, but it did not state it directly. Instead it told a story. The conflict and the crisis of choice which appeared in the dream corresponded to a crisis through which Emma was passing in her life. The dream was thus presenting a picture of the situation within the person. The symbolic style of the psyche was expressed in the fact that this situation was not described in rational and analytical terms, but that it was *portrayed*. It was not stated, but was rather set forth in the form of fictional episodes, complete with action, dialogue, and suspense.

The key to the symbolic style of the psyche is its quality of *dramatization*. Ideas and feelings are personified. They become persons or animals and behave as though they were alive. Most important, the conditions prevailing within the psyche are dramatized in sequences of movement so that the tone of the movement indicates the direction of inward development. Thus, in Emma's dream, the movement of the taxi and the many impediments it encountered portrayed the pattern of events in her life throughout the years. The decision in the taxi, the man at the gate, the phone call to the plane, the renewed opportunity to move ahead, dramatized a change in attitude that was then taking place within her.

Action depicted in a dream involves action taking place at two levels. There is the action occurring in the dream itself; and there is the action going on unseen at a deeper level of the psyche. The action in the dream is the symbolic expression of the action going on in the depths of the psyche. Movement, change, development are continuously taking place at the hidden levels of the personality. Sometimes the movement is so slow that it is barely perceptible; and sometimes it proceeds at a very rapid rate, bringing exhilaration and occasionally disturbance into the life of the individual. Whatever its intensity, however, and whatever its content, movement and change and development are always taking place in the depths of the person, for these comprise the ongoing process by which the psyche fulfills its potentials. The process goes forward beneath the surface of the personality; and when it breaks through to reveal itself on the outer level of experience, as it does in dreams or in other spontaneous forms of expression awake or asleep, it depicts itself in images and dramatizes itself according to the symbolic style inherent in the psyche.

The action in the dream reflects the movement going on in the depths of the psyche. It is this movement that is the effective *reality* of the person. This is the principle that lay behind Emma's feeling that while it was she who had to make the decision, it was the dream that supplied the answer. It would actually have been more accurate to say that the dream disclosed to her the answer that was being worked out without her knowing it in the depths of her psyche. The dream reflected this ongoing process. It served as the medium by which the process could disclose itself, and it portrayed with its dramatic, symbolic style, the course her psyche was seeking to take.

We have here one of the primary principles of the psychology of personal growth. A main function of dreams is to reflect and convey to consciousness the contents and direction of the process working out its next steps at a fundamental depth. This is why dreams have a message, and why, in the oftquoted phrase of the Talmud, "A dream not understood is like a letter not opened." The psyche is in motion, working in its nonconscious darkness to unfold the patterns of experience by which the person can fulfill the meaning of his individual life in the light of consciousness. Its dreams are dramatized messages which give reports in a symbolic style of the progress that is being made in the depth.

If the dream that is dreamt in sleep is remembered on waking, that is usually a sign that something important is taking place in the psyche. If the dream goes un-heeded, or if it is not understood, and if its subject matter remains important, the dream will usually be re-peated, either with the same or with equivalent sym-bols. It seems that if an important part of the process taking place in the depths of the psyche is not recog-nized on the conscious level so that the person cannot cooperate with it and draw it forward in the acts of his life, the process of growth is stymied. The individual then remains in a condition of self-stalemate until he learns to recognize the tendency of his inner life and manages to bring his outer life into accord with it.

IMAGERY AND REFLECTIONS OF INFINITY

A major question is how a person can learn to open the letter of his dream and can learn to read its message, considering that it is written in a veiled, symbolic style. This becomes a difficult task only when it is approached by means of those intellectual theories of psychology that seek to reduce symbols analytically to rational terms. To do this is a distorting act of translation, exemplified in the old Italian phrase, *tradurre e tradire*, to translate is to betray.

The symbolic style of the psyche requires no translation. It can be felt and understood directly in its own terms. It needs no translation provided that the individual has acquired a moderate familiarity with its mode of expression, and a sympathetic feeling for the dimension of inner reality of which it is the medium. In the case of Emma, we saw that no intricate work of analytical deciphering was required. The dream carried its own interpretation for her. She was sensitive to its movement, and so she opened herself to it and permitted herself to go along with it. The meaning of the dream was thus able to reveal itself spontaneously to her. Indeed, the recognition of meaning became a natural continuation of the act of dreaming itself.

It is interesting to note in this connection that knowing the meaning of the dream did not require of Emma that she turn her attention backward to re-experience the events of her childhood. The dream did not relate itself to her past, except in one very significant way. It reconstructed the events in her earlier experience symbolically in capsule form in such a manner that the continuity of events moved into the present and set a perspective in which the possibilities of the future could dramatize themselves. The meaning, or message, of the dream was thus not to be found in its reference to the past but in its forward movement. It was by this for-

ward movement that the way was opened for the dream
to take the next step in unfolding her life.

In this sense, the understanding of dreams does not
require a theory of analytical interpretation, but rather
a sensitivity to their movement and a capacity to participate in their nonconscious flow. The dreams then become facts of experience which express an inward reality, and they serve as instruments by which the psyche
fulfills its function of directing the development of the
individual person.

Movement in the depths of being is the manner in
which the psyche performs its directive role in man. The
content of this movement is imagery, imagery that may
be visual or verbal, auditory, rhythmic, olfactory, intuitive, or generalized in its feeling tone. In all its forms,
the flow of imagery goes on continuously in the psyche, awake or asleep, sometimes implicitly, sometimes
overtly expressed.

The evidence for this is varied and is strongly supported by studies of how creative persons have induced
their inspiration. Recent laboratory researches into the
nature of dream and fantasy also tend to validate the
hypothesis that the flow of imagery is a fundamental
principle of the psyche. The strongest cumulative evidence, however, is provided by the therapeutic method
of *twilight imaging*, some examples of which will be discussed later. Under different names and with several
variations, the literature describing this approach has

immeasurably buttressed the conception of imagery flow.*

In the method of twilight imaging, the individual relaxes, closes his eyes, and permits himself to observe and describe the flow of imagery that moves upon the screen of his mind's eye. This flow, which is a product of the image-making faculty of the psyche, is kaleidoscopic. It simply moves on, presenting itself in one form after another. Its imagery is not integrated, but moves with no apparent cohering principle, until a pattern is formed by the formless flow of the imagery itself. This is the "pure" process of the psyche. To the degree that it is not induced by any selfconscious attitudes, the pattern that is formed and dramatized is an authentic expression of the psyche and reflects what is taking place at its unobservable levels. The free flow of imagery thus becomes a channel by which the inarticulate depths of the person can communicate to consciousness the problems and the aspirations involved in reaching a fuller integration.

The flow of imagery follows the symbolic style of expression that is characteristic of the psyche. Often the images seem to refer to specific persons and events with whom the individual has had recent contact, and at such times there is a strong tendency to interpret the imagery in a literal and matter-of-fact manner. It is im-

---

* Vid., e.g., R. Desoillé, Le Reve Eveille en Psychotherapie, Presses Universitaire de France, Paris, 1945. See also the pamphlet by Roberto Assagioli, Dynamic Psychology and Psychosynthesis, published by the Psychosynthesis Research Fdtn., Greenvale, Del., 1958.

portant then to remember that while many images are nothing more than recalls of environmental contact, and are to that degree of no significance for the development of the psyche, the use of these images by the psyche may hold a symbolic significance that should not be missed. It does no good for the individual then to become self-consciously analytical about the images, but an attitude of openness and sensitivity to the symbolic dimension can be very fruitful at that point. If he permits it to move onward and to speak to him as it moves, the dream and imagery flow will in due course reveal to him whether a particular image is essentially symbolic or is merely environmental. Its significance and its value for him will be indicated to him by the overall symbolic context as this context takes definite shape.

This symbolic context has two main aspects: it expresses the pattern of growth that is characteristic of the person's life as a whole; and it expresses the pattern of imagery required by the formative symbols working in the psyche. The formative symbols have a special importance. Images follow a symbolic style in their movement, but of themselves they are unstructured. The principles of patterning that give structure to the images are the formative symbols. There is a great deal to be said in describing their various dynamic aspects. The formative symbols have a powerful effect as they operate within the psyche. They have the capacity both of releasing tremendous amounts of energy for directed action and of greatly enlarging the faculty of intuitive cognition. Much detail of this has already been set forth in another volume.* Two classifications of the formative symbols are, however, important for the continuity of our present discussion. These are the *Representational Symbols* and the *Elemental Symbols*.

Representational Symbols belong to the social sphere of life. They are formed by combinations of images that draw their meaning from the context of the cultural beliefs in which they arise. Thus the flag of a country is a representational symbol. The uniform of a soldier, the vestments of a priest, the structure of a church, or temple, or mosque, are representational symbols. Intense loyalties are often attached to such symbols and they have the power to unleash great amounts of energy in the form of political and religious events.

Representational symbols may carry a tremendous emotional force in social groups, but their characteristic is that they stand for something definite. The flag, for example, stands for a particular country, a particular people, or a particular political movement. To see it evokes the emotions that accompany the individual's identification and involvement in the group for which the flag stands. The emotional quality is direct, intense, and immediate because the representational symbol has a specific connotation.

Even in the case of religious symbols, such as the

---

* See Progoff, *Depth Psychology and Modern Man*, Chapters 5-9, pp. 107-241.

Cross, the Star of David, or the Crescent, where the point of reference is a religious experience that is highly subjective, the symbol stands for something definite. It stands for a particular type and quality of religious contact as that has been formalized and communicated to the individual in the course of his childhood training. In fact, a large measure of the emotional power of representational symbols comes from the overlay of loyalty which they carry. In modern times we see this especially where religious symbols are concerned. Very often individuals feel cold toward the religious doctrine that a symbol represents, but they are still bound to the symbol emotionally because of their loyalty to the people, the cultural traditions, and their own childhood experiences with which they identify it.

Elemental symbols arise from a quite different aspect of the human psyche. With them, the context of society is relatively unimportant because the main force in them derives from a principle which shapes them and directs their unfoldment from within.

The Elemental Symbols are reflections in man of the primary processes of the universe in their varied phases and aspects. The infinity of the universe encompasses man. It excites his wonder, but it eludes his knowledge. Nonetheless, some quality of its infinity seems to be part of the nature of the human being. It is present in him as the equivalent in human form of the creative principle that pervades the universe. It expresses the kinship of man to the rest of creation. The psyche with its reflecting faculty acts as a mirror for the principles by which the infinity of the universe disperses itself and becomes finite in particular forms and patterns.

The instruments by which this mirroring is done are the Elemental Symbols. These are drawn not from the environment but from the nature of the psyche itself, as the psyche reflects the cosmos. In using the word, "elemental," we mean to indicate that these are symbols whose source is deep in the very ground and tissue of human nature. In fact, the Elemental Symbols are so generically fundamental that it may be more accurate to think of them as principles of symbol formation rather than as fixed symbols in themselves. This aspect of the elemental symbols involves their tendency to act as patterning principles for clusters of images which then become instruments for the unfoldment of meanings that transcend the symbols and images themselves. To understand the implications of this, we shall need the detailed discussions of personal experiences in the illustrative sections that follow. From these, too, we shall be able to draw the important practical consequences that are implicit in the active principle underlying elemental symbols.

The elemental symbols are not definite symbols that can be enumerated and described. By their very nature they cannot be definite symbols because they do not represent something fixed with clearly marked boundaries. A flag, for example, is a definite object and it stands for something specific; as such it is a representational symbol. But an elemental symbol, because of its inherently fluid nature, cannot be concrete. Its quality is not that it stands for something that is now known or has been known in the past. Its characteristic, rather, is that it moves toward something that is not yet known, something which in principle cannot be known in any fixed formulation or concept because its nature is not limited to the finite forms which can be described in the intellectually structured laws of a science.

The elemental symbols involve a reaching and a moving out towards the principles that work behind the finite. They cannot be definite because they are reaching toward *moving* principles. Thus a double motion is involved. The elemental symbols are in motion and that toward which they are reaching is in motion. When this is comprehended and known as a fact and capacity of one's being, the experience that unites this double motion, in the personality and in the cosmos, has a dynamic and transforming effect. We shall be able to look more deeply into this in later chapters where the psychological events in which such encounters take place are described. For example, in Carl's entry into the open spaces in the stones* and in Mrs. White's vision into the depths of existence† we shall see instances of elemental symbols that carry the individual out and past his individuality into a moving and extending connection with life.

* See Chap. IV, Section 1, p. 109.
† See Chap. IV, Section 4, p. 153.

The connection that takes place then is not a static fact. It is not a connection that one gets and then keeps, or just stays with. It is a connection that draws the individual into union with a moving reality. This is a reality that is ever in motion, that enlarges itself by growth in the midst of life. The experience of reaching union with it is thus not an experience of static unity. It does not lead to a mystical ecstasy in which time is stopped for what is subjectively felt as a timeless pleasure, or in which one seems to escape from time. It is rather an experience of active participation in which time opens from within, encompassing the world in the terms of a symbol so that more can be included in it. Involvement in life then becomes more intense, the feeling of it becomes more vivid and more expressive of the many dimensions of reality. It is an experience of enlargement, a participation in the principle that moves in the background of life, entered into by means of an elemental symbol.

This symbolic act of ongoing unity by which the individual is enabled to rejoin the infinite, which is his origin, is an act that is not to be analyzed while it is occurring; for that would stop the process by which it moves forward. Analysis would lead to self-consciousness; and this would inhibit the process by which the meaning and message of the elemental symbols disclose themselves.

It is not to be analyzed, but it is to be extended. That is the spirit and the methodology behind it. Entering into an elemental symbol is like entering a vehicle and being carried along within it. The vehicle of an elemental symbol carries man into dimensions of the infinite where it becomes possible for the meaning of finite human existence to disclose itself. He may not be able to state this meaning, at least not in direct and literal or logically intellectual terms; but the way of it becomes known to him by the very fact of riding in the vehicle. Without his intending it or being aware that it is happening, it becomes a cohering and integrating force in his life. It alters his relation to reality, not as a matter of belief or of rational desire, but by virtue of the fact that he is participating in its ongoingness with a new quality of awareness.

When the symbolic dimension of existence opens itself to an individual, his view of reality is strikingly changed. He perceives things simultaneously on diverse levels. A new comprehension of what reality is then becomes accessible to him. It is not doctrinal, and it is not cast in terms of fixed metaphysical or religious concepts, neither ontological idealism, nor materialism, nor any ideological dogma. It involves, rather, an open and moving relationship to principles of the cosmos, as these are reflected by an elemental symbol in the depths of the psyche. Neutral as far as religious doctrines are concerned, and capable of moving by means of religious symbols when their quality is elemental, it establishes a personal point of contact, based not on hearsay but on the individual's own experience. Meaning enters the existence of modern man, then, by means of experiences within his psyche; for the psyche is the mirror in which the principles of the infinite universe are reflected for the finite person.

DESCRIBING THE BOUNDLESS

We have spoken of the psyche in varying terms, and some of these may appear, on the surface, to be contradictory. Primarily we have described the psyche as the directive principle that guides the development of the individual from the seed of potentiality to the unfoldment of meaningful life. We have also, however, spoken of the psyche in terms of depth, as though it were a place with space in it divided into levels. To be a *principle* and to be a type of *space* may appear to involve contradictories, but these are only two aspects of a many-sided reality which requires a flexible attitude if its paradoxes are to be understood.

What is the spatial aspect of the psyche? In everyday speech it is customary to distinguish between mental contents that are superficial and those that are deep. Colloquially people speak of ideas that come "off the top of the head," in contrast to those that come from the *heart* or the *guts* or the *soul*. Implicitly the distinction is between thoughts that are derived from contact with the environment and thoughts that are drawn from the

depths of the person.* The former have only a fleeting
significance, but the latter are characterized by their
warmth of emotion and the fullness of their concern for
truth. They are not shallow ideas but profound feelings.

This colloquial conception of *depth* implies a value
judgment. What comes from the depth of the person instead of "off the top of his head" carries a stronger impression of authenticity. A commonsense perception
about the nature of the psyche is involved here. Ideas,
feelings, memories which are drawn from contact with
the environment are of more superficial content. They
tend to be subjective, transitory, and of less fundamental import. It appears that there are gradations
within the psyche, that some contents are experienced
as being at a deeper level of the psyche than others. It is
thus that the conception of the psyche has arisen as a
type of space, as a space within the person.

There is a definite pragmatic value in this way of
thinking about the psyche. It makes possible a hypo-
thetical scale by which we can evaluate mental contents
in terms of their closeness to the outer world. Are they,
for example, based upon environmental memories? Are
they wishes? Or repressions? If they are, they belong,
because of their personal subjectivity, to a relatively
superficial level of the psyche. Do they belong, on the

---

* See in this connection, Gardner Murphy, Human Potentialities,
Basic Books, N. Y. 1958 p. 299-301. See also, L. L. Whyte, Aspects
of Form, Indiana University Press, Bloomington.

other hand, to the generic patterns that are universal tendencies in man? Do they touch, or point toward, what is timeless in human experience? If they do, they possess a quality of objectivity that is transpersonal; their source then lies in the fundamental depths of the psyche where the elemental symbols are.

These gradations in the psyche refer to the *qualities* of psychic contents. Those that are subjective tend to be of only passing significance and they belong to the superficial level of the psyche. Those that have the quality of the universal and the transpersonal are of more lasting significance and have their source at a deeper level. The underlying conception here is in terms of the qualities of the psyche, but to speak of depth carries implications of space. It is as though the psyche were a large, spaceless space within the person, a space in which the various levels of experience are contained. And yet we know that the psyche is not actually a container, and that it is not actually a place within man. To speak of it in terms of space seems, however, to enable us to conceive of and to work fruitfully with the dynamic traits of the psyche. In one sense, then, to think of the psyche as a space containing levels of depth is operational and pragmatic.

More fundamentally, however, to speak of depths in the psyche is an allusion to the quality of being by which the unfoldment of the psyche proceeds. It is an attempt to represent and convey a dimension of experience that is otherwise exceedingly difficult to grasp in

conceptual terms. One way to think of it is that since
the psyche functions as the directive principle which
guides the growth of the human organism as a whole,
its *contents* are not contents as such. They are not
things within the psyche; they are rather aspects of a
moving principle. They may, perhaps, best be compared to sparks that shoot off from a large fire and start
little fires of their own. They are derivatives of the process by which the psyche serves as the directive principle
in the person. The images that appear then as the sparks
of the psyche, together with the formative symbols
which set the patterns for the images, are not to be understood as entities in themselves. They are aspects of a
moving principle, and thus are always in motion, never
fixed, but always in flow.

The conception of the psyche as a directive principle,
whose elements are representational and are ever in
movement, refers to the dynamics that are the essence
of the psyche. The depths of psychic space are aspects
of this, and to phrase it in these terms is merely a pragmatic way of conceiving of the place in which the psyche
moves, as a river must have a bed in which to flow.
Moving principle and psychic space, repression, subjectivity, depth, and elemental transpersonality, all are
aspects of the symbolic style by which we seek to touch
the boundlessness which is the reality of human nature.
The conception of the psyche itself is an elemental symbol. It mirrors in its symbolic style the infinity of life
that takes finite form in human existence. It is thus a

symbolic vehicle by which we seek to attain a working knowledge of ourselves as human beings. Since it is symbolic, the knowledge which it provides is never exact, only approximate and sometimes merely metaphoric. That is inherent in it and is both its limitation and its special capacity. The psyche as an elemental symbol is to be understood primarily as a means of approaching a subject matter whose vastness and intangibility takes it beyond the grasp and beyond the competence of ordinary formulations.

This combination of limitation and potentiality which we find in a symbolic conception like the *psyche* is paralleled whenever the search for knowledge is pushed to its ultimate boundaries. In its conception of the psyche, depth psychology is facing a human limitation that has already been faced and is still being lived with by atomic physics where the conception of the atom is concerned. In this connection, commenting upon the difficulties that are encountered in the study of atomic physics, Albert Einstein pointed out that, "Atomic theory could be viewed more as a visualizing symbol than as knowledge concerning the factual construction of matter." *

---

* See Paul Arthur Schilpp, editor, *Albert Einstein, Philosopher-Scientist,* New York, Harper, 1949, p. 19. Our discussion of Einstein is derived from a most significant work-in-progress by Lynn Krug dealing with the life experience of Einstein from the point of view of depth psychology. The parallels between Einstein's work and the process of symbolic unfoldment are most impressive and hold the greatest implications for larger insight into the dynamics of scientific discovery.

The implications of this and its correlation with the interpretation of the psyche are of great significance. The conception of the atom and the development of atomic theory are commonly thought to be literal descriptions of physical reality; but that is not the case at all. As Einstein says, atomic theory does not provide a "factual construction of matter" but a "visualizing symbol." It provides merely an image by means of which the structure of reality can be represented and conceived.

When the human mind approaches a basic problem such as the nature of matter or the nature of the psyche, its observations provide only raw data with which to begin. The observations themselves do not contain, and do not themselves even suggest, the concepts with which the data can be given form and meaning. For example, a stone, or a solid block of wood, does not suggest the moving particles of matter in terms of which the atom is conceived. The conception of the atom does not lie in the wood but in the mind of the person who interprets it. It is an image brought forth from the psyche, and it proves its value by its usefulness in the fruitful interpretation of the raw data. Utimately the test of the image lies in facts of observation, as the image of the universe contained in Einstein's general theory of relativity required an eclipse in 1919 to validate its insight.

Even when an image, as a theory, is verified in a specific case by external evidence, it remains a "visualizing symbol." Its "truth" is not absolute but relative and metaphoric. It is defined by the symbolic terms of the governing image, as the conception of the atom. This is the sense in which Einstein says, "Physics is an attempt conceptually to grasp reality as it is thought independently of its being observed." * Since external observation by the canons of common sense is altogether inadequate, physics has had to reach beneath the surface of the mind for its symbolic constructs. It has gone inward, as Einstein did, for images in which to present its symbolic view of the world, and it has used the intuitive logic of mathematics to verify its inner visions and to apply them to the phenomena as they are observed.

The consequence of this approach of physics is a self-consistent version of reality marked off by the framework of the symbols it is using. At certain points this version of reality is tested by external observation, but its essence lies in the inner logic of its symbolic system. "In this sense," Einstein writes, "we speak of 'physical reality.'" †

Physical reality, as Einstein intends the term, is not the commonsense reality of the physical world. It is not the stone you stub your toe on. Physical reality is rather the self-consistent body of knowledge compiled within the symbol structure of modern physics. It is a reality defined by its framework of imagery. No claim

---

* *Ibid.*, p. 81.
† *Ibid.*, p. 81.

is made that its truth is more than relative and partial; but it greatly extends human knowledge nonetheless.

In a manner that parallels the conception of the physical atom, the conception of the psyche as the principle of direction and the place of depth in man is a "visualizing symbol." As atomic theory moves past the commonsense observation of matter to an image of its inner structure, so the theory of the psyche goes past the outer form of personality. It presents an image of man in terms of directive movement, symbolic patterns, and levels of experience beneath the observable surface of the individual. Using the image of the psyche as a "visualizing symbol" makes it possible to reach into the inner structure of personality to identify its principles and processes, its cycles and rhythms. We perceive a continuity of events taking place, and these constitute the "reality" of the psyche.

"Psychic Reality" refers to the category of phenomena taking place in the depths of the psyche when the psyche is conceived as a working symbol in whose terms these phenomena can be consistently interpreted. Psychic reality in this sense is comparable and parallel to Einstein's conception that physical reality refers to the body of concepts that interpret the phenomena of the world *as it is thought* in terms of the symbols of modern physics. Just as atomic physics opened access to a dimension of reality that had not been experienced before and made tremendous amounts of new energy available to man, the symbolic conception of the depths of the psyche opens great new powers of personality and sources of personal strength. These sources of strength are needed, ironically enough, to save us from the threat of destruction which the discoveries of atomic physics brought forth.

The parallel between physics and depth psychology runs as far as the symbolic nature of their primary concepts and their capacity to set energy free; but there it ends. The quality of their application is different. Both lead to a body of knowledge regarding their special segment of reality, but the conception of *psychic reality* leads to more than intellectual knowledge. It leads to disciplines for developing larger capacities of personal experience and a fuller participation in dimensions of reality that reach beyond the individual.

These disciplines are of two general types. They are procedures that may be used by a professionally trained individual in *evoking* from another person a fuller realization of the potentialities latent in the psyche; and they are methods that may be followed by individuals in their privacy working to carry through and extend their awareness of what is ultimately real in existence. We turn now to examine instances of both these procedures in the lives of modern persons.

4 Ways of growth in modern persons

CARL'S ENTRY INTO SPACELESS SPACE

One of the distinguishing characteristics we have observed about modern man is the distance he feels himself to be from traditional forms of religious contact. The dimension of the sacred, which such historians of religion as Mircea Eliade have found to be of major importance, seems strange to the contemporary person. At best he feels uneasy with it. To say this is not to state an opinion, nor is it to pass judgment; it is simply to call attention to a fact that is of the greatest consequence both for our civilization and for the individual personality.

On one level we may ask whether the sensitivity to the dimension of the sacred can be restored by reopening the roads that lead back to the traditions of the past. Psychologically there are many indications that even if it were desirable to make such a return, it would not be feasible in the long run. The modern person who earnestly seeks a meaningful spiritual encounter requires a new, non-traditional style of experience to evoke the timeless in himself. He requires a new way by which he can reach out in freedom. Above all, he requires a methodology that is open and unfettered by prior commitments, so that he can go exploring in the depths of being. He needs to be able to know that whatever he discovers as truth is validated not by external authority but by the quality of his own experience.

In this perspective, the first criterion for a new method is that it will enable the individual to explore freely in the depths of the psyche. He should not become engaged in merely recalling events of the past, but he should become capable of entering areas of awareness and perceiving dimensions of meaning that had not opened to him before. A new psychological method should extend the individual's relation to reality in the largest sense of the term including the ultimates of existence. It should enable him to penetrate deeply into the elemental levels of the psyche where egotism and its accompanying anxieties overcome themselves, and where intimations of transpersonal meanings in life can begin to be felt.

In the nature of things in a civilization whose scale of values deflects the individual away from inward concerns, most people will not undertake the free exploration of the depths of the psyche unless they need to. They seldom choose it willingly, but mainly they enter the process of personal growth only when they are toppled into it. Because of outward difficulties they turn inward, and it is then that the truly major discoveries of life become possible for them. We thus have the situation, which is only superficially a paradox, that the methodology for personal growth and larger spiritual awareness derives from studies and practices whose origin lies in the field of medical therapy. The individual comes for healing of a specific symptom and finds, much to his surprise, that it is the whole person that is involved in the therapy; he learns that the realization of a new quality of being is necessary to effect the psychological cure by which his neurotic symptoms will be eliminated.

The typical situation is that an individual begins with a problem of personal behavior, a problem that is diagnosed, at least in his own mind, as a type of neurosis. He comes for therapeutic treatment in medical terms, and finds in the course of his treatment that an awareness of larger meaning in life enters his experience. This serves as the curative factor because the so-called neurosis was largely a result of the absence of this experience. It resolves the immediate problem, or establishes a context in which it can eventually be solved; but much more important, it opens a psychological capacity for a continuing and growing relation to the elementals of life.

An instance of this process is the life-experience of Carl, a man in his early forties who felt himself to have reached an impasse in his life. Carl was a businessman, but his career in business seemed to have come to a standstill. He was concerned about himself because he was conscious of increasing feelings of physical tension. He realized that he often thought of himself as being inferior to others. He said that he was unable to relate to other persons with the openness that he felt was possible for him. In his attitudes he was in many ways a stereotype of the modern businessman; not a believer in any particular religion, skeptical about all doctrines, matter-of-fact, conservative in his views on morality and social relations.

When we began our talks, he freely told me about his childhood, especially about his early family situation. This part of our conversation sounded well rehearsed, as though he had thought about it in these terms many times before. He described things to me with the kind of psychoanalytical jargon that many persons acquire from newspapers and parlor talk, since we live, as has frequently been observed, in a "psychological era." He interpreted for me how his inhibitions and inferiority feelings had developed, and then he said, well, this is where he found himself.

We discussed his self-analysis, and he soon realized that these conscious theories of his were little more than gleanings from the popular psychological literature he had read. They were of little use to him. Much as he "knew" of the analytical reasons for his difficulties, his apparent knowledge only bound him to his problem more tightly. It certainly did not increase the resources at his command. It did not free him. It did not make him more alert, nor did it place any additional energy at his disposal. He agreed with me that analysis at least as he had practiced it on himself was only a cord he had tied around himself. Something else was needed to open the flow of life within him.

I asked Carl to lie back and let himself relax as fully as he could. He closed his eyes, and I suggested that a screen would appear before his mind's eye and that images would appear upon this screen. There would also be sounds, perhaps words, feelings, and intimations of various kinds. There would be many things that would appear to him, and as they came before him he was to report them to me.

I explained to Carl that though this procedure is referred to as "twilight imaging," much more than visual images would come to him in the course of it. It involves essentially an open reverie conducted at a twilight level, intermediate between waking and sleep. The material that comes to the fore in it is therefore directly connected to the nonconscious depths, but it has the advantage of flowing freely in the midst of consciousness. When the proper rapport is established as the base for twilight imaging, it is like having a deep dream where the elusive contents are not forgotten and lost but are described, shared, and recorded in the moment when they occur. It has the effect of loosening and stimulating the flow of the nonconscious levels of personality, thus generating a momentum of feeling that breaks through the impasse of self-conscious analytical attitudes. It also has the effect of deepening the contact with the self so that many intuitive and even poetic experiences occur, as we shall see, even in persons who are accustomed to nothing more than a superficial perception of life.

Carl was interested in the description of the new procedure and willing to go ahead with it. He lay back on the sofa, closed his eyes, turned his attention inward, watched, and waited. Presently an antelope appeared on the screen facing a high sheer wall. It was a precipice. The antelope became smaller and in a moment disappeared.

The imagery began again, but this time more generalized. There were various geometric forms, one after another. A huge arc formed. Behind it a parabola dimly took shape. There was a feeling of elevators going up and down. Suddenly there was a feeling of reaching out into a broad, expansive area. Carl could not see anything, but he had the sensation of his body being suspended in the air. He was going out into this open vastness as though he were carried in a balloon. There was no fear; it was a pleasant sensation. There was just a free, lifting movement, proceeding at an easy lazy pace, and yet seeming to consume the distance remarkably well. The feeling was of going up, far up, in relation to nothing in particular, no scenery, just rising, pleasantly rising with nothing to see.

In a moment the image changed again. Carl found himself now on a dusty, flat plain. A statue was there, draped in cloth. Then Carl had a strange sensation. It was as though he felt himself entering the cloth. His body was borne, twisting, spiralling in an oblique upward angle. It seemed that somehow he was being carried inside the figure of the statue.

Only at this point did Carl become aware of what the statue was. He felt it to be the figure of an ancient Greek. The statue was bearded. He held a staff in his right hand and a tablet of stone in his other hand. "It could be one of the gods," Carl said. He was quite definite in saying, when I asked him, that he was sure it was a Greek figure. It was not Mosaic. He did not feel an Old Testament quality in it.

Now the figure seemed to rise high in the air. It was still a statue. Far below it there were many very thin mountain peaks, and at the bottom as in a valley there was a bowl-shaped area filled with water. The water was glistening.

The statue began to tilt forward. It seemed to be off

balance, as though there was something unstable about it. Now the base of the statue was descending against a dark background. It was coming down close to the peaks of the mountains. The size of the statue was enormous, bigger than the mountain peaks. It continued sliding and drifting downward, and finally it landed softly. It was like a great stone slab that had come to rest in a very quiet valley.

Next Carl saw something taking off like a rocket. He seemed to be running next to it. It was rising very rapidly, and Carl was going up alongside it. Now he seemed to be encountering a dark mass up at the top of something. It was like "a dark pancake." "But I don't feel that I'm going to crash into it," Carl said.

Now he seemed to have reached the peak of a mountain. It was the high point, thin, shiny white. He had come to rest on it. A thin ring of light was around it now, like an arc. Carl had a feeling of drifting slowly downward, not falling, "just drifting like a leaf." There was a feeling of going up and then down, an upward thrust and a lazy falling back, again and again.

At this point I called the imaging to a halt. Carl had been deep in it. I asked him how he felt. "It's like recovering from dizziness," he said. He felt as though he had been far away, and he felt very much rested, as though he had had a good sound sleep that had lasted much more than the half hour of the imaging session; he had, of course, been awake all the time. He got up and as he began to walk away he remarked that the tenseness he had felt in his body when he had lain down seemed now to have disappeared.

When he came in for his next session, Carl had something he wanted to discuss. He wanted to tell me about his impressions after the previous session.

"It was very interesting," he said. "I woke up, and I didn't realize how far into a semi-trance I had gone. I guess I had been too aware of your note taking and of the tape recorder going. And I was also very much aware of the implications of the fact that I was seeing these images. That was amazing me. I was not completely out yonder, although the images were."

"Then," Carl went on, "after I left you, I went into the bathroom outside your office. I looked in the mirror. I think I am one of the few persons who can pass a mirror without mugging. Even when I shave I don't see myself. But this time I looked to see who I was. It was a strange and interesting experience. I wasn't smiling. There wasn't any particular expression on my face. It was just a face immobile. I got a completely new slant on myself from it. I stared steadily into the eyes, very intently. I was trying to see what was in back of the face. It was as though I might be a stranger, or someone I wanted to know. I really have never looked at myself that way before. It was a very strange feeling."

I asked Carl what he had seen.

"I was looking with an intense searching, just looking into the eyes. There was no smile or any other expression to distract me from what I could see. I don't really know exactly what I saw except that I felt a certain exhilaration. Perhaps it was the aftereffects of having been in that imaging state. I don't know. I saw a lot of wear and tear that I hadn't realized was evident on my face. It's as though I was trying to find out who was behind the eyes."

"What did you find behind the eyes?" I asked Carl.

"Well, I guess I was still feeling the imagery state I had been in. Something that was not me had put those images there. I guess I was looking for whatever it was that brought those images up. I was looking for something like that."

Carl continued. "I think I wanted to see what was really there. It's funny, but it's as though there was something poetic about it in some way. There was a feeling of something stirring in me. It was a huge stirring upward. Whatever that stirring was, I was it. Whatever was stirring was me. But it was not as a form or as a face that I saw in the mirror. It was just a sort of knowing that it was I myself that was stirring. And then together with that there was a very steady feeling. Very quiet. I felt there was a solidity. And funny, but I felt quite confident looking into myself. I felt that there was a lot of material on tap. I didn't feel trapped at all as I have been feeling. I had a feeling of connection with something quite deep, something that was beyond the eyes there in the mirror. I had a feeling of a lot of energy that was waiting to do things, wanting to do things."

We discussed what this feeling was and what it implied. What had happened in the imaging? He had lain down full of his habits, his thoughts of the day, thoughts of his problems, and all the other distractions that fill the conscious mind. Gradually as he had become aware of the images appearing before his mind's eye, his attention had been absorbed by the images, and he had forgotten himself. The feeling then was of drifting down, going deep, and being far away. It was as though something else or someone else was working within him. The flow of imagery expressed the principle of the psyche itself moving at its elemental, unguided depths beyond the influence of his special environmental situation, beyond his habits and his thoughts. The movement of images proceeded from the place in the psyche that is not reached by distractions coming from the outward senses.

It was the pure flow of the psyche that was involved, his naked, unconditioned self. The complete dropping off of conscious control inherent in the imaging process had stirred a feeling of that real self within him. When he had gotten up and had gone into the washroom, his first spontaneous prompting had been to make that self tangible, to *see* this real, naked, true self that had created these amazing images without his conscious participation. He looked for his real self in the mirror, the self beyond his face, what the Zen Buddhists would speak of as the original face he had before he was born; or what the anonymous author of *The Cloud of Unknow-*

ing would call his "Naked Being." And the feeling that this true self gave him was a good and appropriate one, a feeling of solidity and strength, of energy and capacity.

In the sessions that followed we continued to use the twilight imaging procedure with a variety of results. Carl found himself becoming increasingly free as he moved about in the depths of himself, observing and listening, and discovering the richness of being that stirred within him, a richness that he did not create but that provided awareness and sensitivity out of its own nature. Sometimes the imaging began with a dream. On those occasions I would read the dream to Carl as he had reported it to me. I would read it while his eyes were closed and he was drifting back down into the dream so that he could continue and extend it. Sometimes we would begin with the contents of a previous imaging session. On those occasions Carl would lie back, close his eyes and drift back into the previous imaging situation while I recreated the atmosphere of it by reading from my notes. At other times we would simply begin with nothing, no previous image or dream, relying on nothing but the free flow of the psyche moving in its natural element of depth.

One of the images that recurred to Carl most frequently was the antelope. In our conscious discussions he was able to identify it as a figure that had fascinated him some years back. He had in fact done a satisfying painting of it when he was in his middle teens. It was

one of the few paintings he had kept from his high
school years, for he had done no art work of any kind
after that. Associating freely on the image of the antelope Carl had identified its free natural strength, its
litheness, capacity for strong, graceful, uninhibited
movement. He also identified it with the time in his
life when he was functioning at his best. He had won
many honors when he was in high school, and his elders
had seen in him at that time a promise of excellence and
achievement which he had not been able to fulfill. The
antelope was therefore a symbol to him of the unfulfilled promise of his life, and of the abundant natural
capacity still roaming free and unharnessed within him.
It was a productive image when Carl called it up at the
beginning of an imaging session, and he used it to begin
a session on several occasions.

At one particular session Carl began with the figure
of the antelope upon the screen of his mental vision.
Its presence drew him down into the atmosphere of the
imagery level, and he felt a close and warm connection
with the antelope. This came quickly, but in a moment
the image of the antelope disappeared. In its place there
came the statue he had seen before, the impressive
Zeus-like stone statue of the figure he felt to be a Greek
god.

As the image of the statue appeared before him, Carl
felt a strong pull toward it. He described it as a feeling
of "some kind of spiritual power in the statue." "There
is something there that is attracting me, drawing me,"

Carl said. "It's as though he has the power of a god. It's a very moving feeling."

At this point, however, Carl lapsed. He slipped out of the dark flow of the imagery and spoke self-consciously of what he was doing. He began to analyze its meaning, and he said that perhaps this sensation of drawing and attraction which he felt meant that he wished his father, who had died several years before, were still alive. He thought that perhaps he missed his father more than he had known and that the figure upon his mental screen was nothing but a father-image.

As he was speculating this way, self-consciously and analytically, Carl slipped further and further from the quality of contact that had characterized the beginning of the imaging session. He had gone back into an analytical attitude, and this had broken the connection. It had spoiled the sense of power that had begun to be communicated to him by the figure of the antelope and by the stone statue of the god.

I remarked to Carl that it might very well be true that a nostalgic yearning for his father was an element in this experience. It undoubtedly was part of the emotional tone of it, and it certainly was an important factor in the background of his total psychological situation. But was it a dynamic factor? Did it have a creative tendency? The flow of imagery to which our sessions had begun to give momentum was part of a process of growth in his psyche as a whole. It involved a forward movement, a movement in the direction of a larger fulfillment of his personality, and the symbols it used were vehicles of this. To interpret these symbols in terms of the past situation out of which the process of growth was moving had the effect of reducing them to the past and fastening his psyche there. What was important, I said, was to maintain the feeling of flow in the psyche and to permit ourselves to participate in it and assist it as it sought to move forward. Could we try again, and attempt to return to the depth level of our twilight imaging now without detouring ourselves?

Carl understood this point on the basis of our previous experiences together. He had already recognized the fact that self-conscious, self-analytical habits of thinking have surreptitiously become part of many persons' minds as a result of the popularization of Freudian psychology; and he understood that when these habits assert themselves their effect is to inhibit the forward flow of the psyche. On one occasion we had discussed this in a general way, and at that time we had seen in it one of the main reasons that artists became disenchanted with psychoanalysis after their first flurry of enthusiasm. They had discovered then that the analytical attitude of psychology constricts the free flow of inspiration coming from deep levels of the psyche. Psychoanalysis and its variations had therefore produced interesting intellectual theories but not great creative art.

Carl had underscored this view when we had discussed it. He had already had sufficient experience of imaging to know the nature and validity of the process and the importance of the symbolic material it brings to the surface. At that time he had expressed the strong feeling that there must in principle be a significant parallel between the creative development of his relatively average personality and the process of the psyche that brings forth creative works in the various fields of art. He was therefore quite willing to regard his foray into self-conscious analysis as a deterrent and distraction in our work. It was the reassertion of an old habit in his thinking, a habit which he would avoid in the future, at least when he was seeking to contact the depths of his personality. He closed his eyes again and began the twilight imaging anew.

In a moment the statue of the Greek god reappeared upon the screen of his mind's eye. He became aware again of the quality of inner power that was in the figure. There was something nonpersonal now about what he felt. It was, he said, somehow "a real soul power."

The statue remained upon the screen and Carl found himself becoming increasingly fascinated by its eyes. The eyes seemed to be the source of the power he felt in the statue. "It's odd," Carl said, "but I feel something that is truly myself functioning here. It's not physical. It's as though something at the very core of myself was involved in this. I feel it in myself, and I feel it in the god in the statue, whoever he is. It is as though the power in him goes together with the power in me. It's as though that's the reason I can feel the power in him.

Because it is in me. But it's not a personal power. It's a universal power in some way. It's hard to explain because it's mainly a feeling. But it's real."

Carl was silent for a moment. Then he continued. "The eyes are affecting me very much now. The power is in them especially. It's as though the statue has a kind of all-seeing vision. Not physically, but an all-seeing vision because of his soul power. Somehow the feeling is that this is a power that I have, too. Also the all-seeing vision is present in me.

"I feel myself reaching out for this power. I'm reaching toward it. It's an effort; but it's an effortless effort. It's as though I'm freed to reach for this power."

"What freed you?" I asked.

"That was almost instantaneous with getting into the feeling of the imagery," Carl replied at once.

We stopped the imaging session at this point in order to discuss it briefly. I asked Carl what was the primary thing he had felt in the imaging.

"The first word that comes to my mind," he said, "is freedom." He went on to say then as soon as he was fully in the stream of the imaging, feeling himself in the psychic atmosphere of depth in which it took place, he felt free. He felt, that is to say, that the walls surrounding his life, the walls that enclose him and constrict him, had dropped away. He was free to move. He was free to be. He was free to live as his inner nature might wish.

The image of the antelope became important to him

at this point. It expressed natural energy that was free in its expression. He knew, he said, that what he felt in this imagery was this kind of freedom. But what this freedom meant to him, Carl added, was the capacity to develop himself and to succeed in life. It represented the promise he had felt in himself when he was in his late teens. It was a promise which he had thought was lost altogether and was impossible of fulfillment. Now, however, he felt free to feel it again, and with a quality that made it seem possible to attain. Perhaps this was why the feeling of power in the statue had been so strong.

No, Carl quickly corrected himself at this point. The power he had felt in the statue was not simply life energy and the potentiality of success in life. It was something more. It was something different. It had really quite another quality. It was soul power. That seemed to be the only phrase with which Carl could feel satisfied in describing it.

This soul power which came from the eyes of the stone statue was very strong, more than personal, and yet very intimate. In the session Carl had had the definite feeling that he was able to sense or recognize this power in the statue because it was a power that he himself possessed. This seemed to him to be a strange thought and he could not develop it further at that time. But it seemed tremendously important to him, and tremendously significant. We left it as an open question.

At the next session of twilight imaging, the figure of the antelope was again the first upon the screen. This time, however, the antelope was a statue. It remained still, was quite large, and for a moment dominated the entire field of mental vision. A second figure then appeared next to the antelope. Carl described it as a carved figure "gracefully vertical and bathed in light." He seemed to be trying to reject this second image, as though he were struggling to avoid it.

"It seems to have arms or wings stretched outward," he reported. "I can't tell which." Carl hesitated here, caught in the midst of the struggle with the image, and finally he said, "I don't really believe in angels or sculptured images or icons, but it seems to be persisting. There it is. I guess I may as well accept it as one of the images."

He continued. "There is a ray of light going vertically from the figure. It is arched slightly to the right at the top, going rather high up. I seem to want to proceed upwards on this path of light. No, I don't think I will go. But I seem to want to go upwards. I'm holding back though; it's as though I want to make sure the path of light is real.

"Somehow I am being drawn up the path of light anyway. It goes way up, and I have nothing to do with it. I am just being drawn up. There at the top is a stone. It is a rather large rectangular block of stone. It is light gray in color. It seems quite clear, and it is strong in my vision, but now it is receding a bit. Now it is getting stronger and clearer, and now it seems to be receding again. It's back again, clearly, and I can see it.

"It seems to me that the stone is the base of a statue, and I have the feeling that the statue is the one I encountered last time. It was the statue of the Greek god figure, the Zeus-like one. But I don't see the upper part of the statue; I see only the base now. It's just that I have a sort of intimation of a statue up above it. I have a feeling that the statue above is going to be shown to me." There was a pause here. Carl was apparently looking and waiting, expecting to see the upper part of the statue with the god figure. It did not appear to him, however, and at length he continued.

"I have been looking at the stone block at the base of the statue expecting that the upper part of the statue would appear. But nothing has appeared. I find that all this time I have just been looking at the stone block very intently. I have been sort of concentrating on it, and now I have a very strange feeling. I feel myself to be within the stone. It is strange because my physical body doesn't seem to be affected, or even involved. The block of stone is the same as it was physically; that is, it is still as hard as rock just as it was, but something about it is different. The stone seems to be composed of a lot of loosely related white particles, and somehow there seems to be a lot of room among them. It's these open spaces that I seem to be able to enter. It's because of these open spaces within the structure of the stone that

I can be within the stone. But it has nothing to do with the physical structure of the stone. There are no holes in the stone. It is solid. And I am within it, but I am not physically within it. It's as though there is some quality in me that is like the open spaces in the stone, and it is because of this common quality that I can enter the stone."

Carl paused now. He was obviously involved in a large and moving vision about which he could communicate only a very small part. There before me he was in the act of experiencing it, and at the same time trying to describe it.

"I have a sudden insight," he said suddenly. "It's a revelation to me that this is actually entry into the periphery of the God power. It seems to me that I am now part of the molecular structure of the stone. I have practically no knowledge about the patterns of molecular structure, but I think I have heard molecules described as having fairly wide separations within them. Well, I feel that I am somewhere in the molecular structure of the stone. This is where I must be. The insight that strikes me, that shakes me, is that God seems impenetrable, impossible to embrace, until we permit ourselves to co-mingle with the substance of God or God power. Then it is effortless. There is nothing to do. We are simply within it. This is how I feel now. I feel within it."

I asked Carl to try to describe more of what he was feeling.

"It's a feeling that is very difficult to put into words,"

he said. "I was going to say that it is entering the space within the substance of God. That seems to fit what I feel, but I don't know what the substance of God is or what it means as a phrase. What I feel is that there is a God substance in the stone, and this is very different from the hard stoniness of the stone. It is the open spaces in the stone; that is the God substance, if I use that phrase for it. It is something one can co-mingle with, in the very substance of it; become one with the very substance of it. It's not like going in or going out or going around it or taking it to yourself; but it's just becoming part of it. That seems to be possible; that seems to be happening because the open spaces are a sort of God quality in the stone, and there is something in me that I feel that has this quality too, this open spacedness within me; and it is this openness, or even emptiness because they are empty spaces, that makes the entry into the stone, and the uniting with the stone possible."

I asked Carl if there seemed to be more to the image.

He answered that the entire imaging had a quality of movement and of continuity. He had been ascending along a shaft of light when he had come to the stone and had thought it to be the base of a statue. There his experience of union with the inner parts of the stone had come to him, but the implication of the imaging was that this was only one aspect of a much larger process. The light was continuing to move upward. Now, however, it had become two shafts of light, two very narrow shafts of light, moving parallel and exceedingly close to each other. They were going straight upward, absolutely straight, higher and higher upward. Very, very high up on these shafts of light, very high up, there seemed to be a small platform made of stone.

At this point again Carl had a feeling of wanting to ascend. At first he did not move in the imagery, but in a moment he was going upward along the two parallel shafts of light. He felt himself moving upward, upward, until he reached the small stone platform that was held high up on the shafts of light. Carl then stepped on the platform and stayed on it, but the platform itself moved. It moved up and up along the two shafts of light. Now the shafts of light approached an especially vivid area. It was filled with brightness. There was the question of whether this was where the movement upward had been heading. Was this the destination and goal of the shafts of light? Was something final to be revealed to him now? There was an excitement and expectancy in the imaging now, as though it were reaching an ultimate culmination. But no, this was not a culmination, and the implication was that there was not to be one. Here was an especially luminous place, but it was not an ending. The shaft of light would continue going up and up, further and further, taking the platform on which Carl stood along with it. It would go on and on in its ascent, infinitely high and endlessly. There was not a conclusion, but an ever-extending movement upward.

At this point, while Carl was filled with the power of his experience and feeling the impact of its implications, we brought our session of twilight imaging to a close.

At our next meeting, Carl began by describing to me the more prosaic effects of the session. "I left the office with a slight tingling and feeling of bigness in my body," he said. "When I had arrived at the office before the session my shoulders had been tight and tense. As I left the office and for some time afterwards I tried consciously to feel this tenseness in my body, but I could not. It is not there. It seemed to me a very dramatic change from a tension that had been with me for several days and had been very painful. It had really hurt, but it wasn't there after the session."

Carl then went on to describe an aftereffect of the session that was of much greater implication. "When I walked out of the office," he said, "my attention was drawn to the sky. It seemed particularly nice. I found myself feeling very calm despite all the problems that I have had to think about lately. I walked along very unhurried, though I did have an appointment to go to; and I felt especially kindly toward all the strange faces on the street. I felt very close to them, as though I knew them intimately in some way without actually knowing them at all. It was a very good warm feeling. I was obviously deeply relaxed, physically and in every way, more than I could understand.

"In fact," Carl added, "when I started to drive home and was on the Parkway, there was tremendous confusion on the road. There were tie-ups everywhere, but I was able to drive without feeling any agitation at all. As the cars were jammed bumper to bumper, I was even able to have a warm feeling for the people in the other cars. But I guess every time I have these images I become much more relaxed, and in a quiet way I feel a certain exhilaration."

We turned our discussion back to his imagery experience of the block of stone. I asked Carl about the solidity of the stone and about the feeling he had of space.

"At first it was just a block of stone," he said. "The next impression I had was that I had somehow gone inside the stone. I had had no difficulty in doing so. It had simply happened, and I felt it clearly. The block still felt solid, but it was composed of loosely held particles. I was not really penetrating them; I was just within the block by means of the empty spaces."

"Was there room?" I asked. "How many could be there?"

"A great many could be there simultaneously without being crowded," Carl answered directly. "It is definitely not in terms of a material figure. I feel it *not as a body but as an awareness.*"

That last phrase was spoken with considerable difficulty. Carl was obviously groping for a way of describing this virtually indescribable experience that had come to him. He knew it to be a reality because it had happened to him. But how could he communicate it in a way that would enable me to know what he had perceived? A real difficulty was involved here. It depended to a considerable degree on the empathy, the sympathetic rapport and understanding, that had developed in our relationship. More than that, if we were to extend his experience and draw forth its implications, it was necessary that I enter with him into the dimension of reality which he was now encountering.

What was Carl trying to communicate when he described the spaces in the stone "not as a body but as an awareness?" He felt it as a nonphysical space, as a spaceless space. But could he call it "spiritual space"? The word, "spiritual," presented a problem to him, as it does to many modern people. Nonetheless, he spoke of the open spaces in the stone as possessing an "element of God power." I asked him why he related it to God, and he said that the open spaces in the stone seemed to possess the ineffable, transcendent quality he identified with God. He could not explain that any further, but the validity of it and its importance to him were apparent facts.

SYMBOLIC AWARENESS OF THE REAL

Carl seemed to be stretching himself inwardly. It was as though he were trying to stretch an indefinite distance from a specific point where his consciousness now rested to a place which he knew existed but which he could not exactly locate. It was not a wide gap but an elusive one, and difficult to bridge because of that. The events that transpire in the depth of the psyche have their characteristic style and mode of expression, and this is very different in tone from the events of outer experience. In the world of sensory experience, space has definite qualities. Its qualities are fixed and constitute its finiteness. Two objects, for example, cannot be in the same space at the same time. On the other dimension, the dimension of symbolic experience, however, these limitations do not prevail. Here it is a spaceless space, a space that is not limited by qualities of physical finiteness.

These two aspects seem to contradict each another; and yet, in a larger perspective, they do not conflict at all. Carl's experience had placed a conundrum before him, comparable in its implications to the *Koans* set by the Zen Buddhist masters. These *Koans* are problems given to the Zen neophytes who come seeking spiritual enlightenment.[*] They are problems whose solution transcends rationality, even to the point of breaking rationality apart by rendering it useless as a way of knowing. The *Koans* are a traditional form of discipline within Zen Buddhism designed to bring about a larger spiritual awareness; but in Carl's case a comparable process was brought into operation directly and autonomously by the activity that had been stimulated in the depth of his psyche.

There is here an important characteristic of the meth-

* D. T. Suzuki, *Zen Buddhism*, Anchor Books, Chapter 6.

ods used in depth psychology that holds the greatest practical implications for spiritual growth among modern individuals. The procedures of depth psychology, especially as aspects of *twilight imaging* are brought into play, touch and activate the same depth dimension of the psyche that has been reached by advanced spiritual disciplines in the history of religion. Depth psychology, however, as a modern spiritual discipline, does not rely upon traditional ways that belonged to cultures of the past in which the uniqueness of the individual was blurred by conformity to ritual practice. Its source, rather, is the integral depths of each individual psyche, for it follows the inherent pattern and tempo of the individual personality in evoking from the depths of the psyche a contact with reality that reaches beyond the contradictories of life.

Struggling with the contradictions, Carl felt that their effect was to draw him toward an awareness of unity that seemed so tangible he could almost touch it. The tension of the conflicting dimensions, the physical and spiritual aspects of space, seemed to open a new sensitivity in him, enabling him to make entry into another kind of place, which seemed to be another level or dimension of human experience. It was in this sense that Carl felt that his entry into the open spaces of the stone was "not as a body but as an awareness."

His co-mingling with the structure of the stone represented for him an opening of understanding that went beyond his conscious understanding. By means of it he knew more than he could understand. It was simply a fact that the continuity of his imagery experience had deposited him in the midst of a quality of consciousness which he had not experienced before. With it there came a suffusion of meaning that connected him with the innermost parts of the stone. It enabled him to feel his kinship with the hidden parts of the natural world.

Carl made the interesting remark in the course of our discussion that the stone seemed to him to be a most elemental object; nothing could be simpler than a stone. It was thus for him, he felt, a symbol of the ultimate and most basic aspects of life. If he could penetrate the hidden parts of a stone, and become one with it, he could penetrate anything and blend with it. Carl referred to a feeling within him now which he could describe only as "boundlessness." "I have the feeling now," he said, "that I understand what lies behind the experience of all those persons in history who have expressed a basic insight about life.

"Each is valid. But it must be that as they articulated it or interpreted their experience they may have promulgated a restricted and closed-circuit religion, and that was faulty. But I know what they touched that lies behind the doctrines, whatever the doctrines were. And that is true.

"Actually," Carl continued, "I think I have at least a hint now of the real feeling in the life of Albert Schweitzer. What I feel is not just an admiring sympathy for his way of life, but I think I have a glimpse of how it might feel to be like this. I feel that I know what it is really to love regardless of the faith or form or behavior of a stranger. I think," he was speaking slowly and reflecting at this point, "I think it has to do with the God particles which were the open spaces in the stone. They are present in the most humble being, like the stone, and they are in the most noble of us. We are truly of a oneness in this sense. We can look at anyone and see the visible person on the outside and at the same time see the particles of open space within. It is impossible to hate these particles. They don't have enough substance to be a target. That must be why Schweitzer could be as he is. I understand his 'reverence for life' now. It's a recognition of the sameness of the open spaces in others, and a joining with them."

At the depth where he was now, Carl's experience possessed a quality of meaningfulness that validated itself within its own terms. It was not a belief that had come to him about the unity of life. It was not a conscious opinion inclining him to be in favor of loving his fellow man. It was a fact of experience. It was something he felt as a reality of his being, a reality that had *happened* to him in the depth of his psyche and had become a fact of his existence.

There is a very significant similarity between the *place* where Carl's experience occurred and the sacred space which Mircea Eliade has identified as the abiding fact in the history of religions. As a result of broad researches into the religious experience of many cultures,

Eliade has demonstrated the importance of the ritual event of initiation in which the death of the individual and his rebirth are symbolically enacted.* He has shown that whether it is the initiation of a teen-age boy into the mysteries of the hunter group, or the initiation of a medicine man into the higher mysteries of the tribe, the goal is a transformation of consciousness that enables the initiated one to enter a larger dimension of reality.

To achieve this, he is brought by means of the ritual to a level of experience where the gods, the primordial, power of the tribe, are felt to live out their timeless lives. This is the dimension from which the tribe derives its models of behavior, its ultimate truth and the holy wisdom that is transmitted from generation to generation. It is the dimension of sacred space and sacred time; but Eliade's point, and the point of many commentators, is that man in the modern age no longer recognizes this dimension of reality and is no longer capable of entering sacred space. Nonetheless, Carl's journey by means of imagery possessed the qualities of an initiation spontaneously experienced. By means of images drawn from the depth of the psyche, Carl entered sacred space and recognized it as being not a physical place but a spaceless place, the place where an awareness of realities that are beyond the range of ordinary vision and ordinary experience becomes possible. With unpremeditated im-

* See Mircea Eliade: *Cosmos and History; The Sacred and the Profane; Birth and Rebirth; Myth, Dream and Mysteries.*

agery befitting a man of our age of science, Carl went to the place where the neophyte goes in a primitive ritual if he is to become one of the initiated ones who *know* spiritual reality. He then becomes capable of knowing things with a profundity and intensity that had not been his before he had been brought to the sacred place.

To primitive tribes, and to the vast majority of historical religions, the belief that one has gone to a special place for one's inspiration is understood as a literal fact. This is indeed an understandable belief, because the psychological experience usually involves a sensation of traveling that is so vivid and strong that it suggests physical reality. Going "down" into the psyche is felt inwardly as a journey, a journey that may go either down or up. A deep dream often represents it so; and in Carl's imagery experience, he was brought upward by two shafts of light that carried the platform on which he stood. It was thus that he came psychologically to the other place where the new awareness became possible. This is the place where one can enter the realm of the spiritual mysteries, the realm where stones have open spaces.

In cultures other than ours the journey to this place is embellished with many symbolic beliefs. It is considered a holy journey, and the sacred place to which one goes is hallowed. A modern man like Carl, however, could not conceivably understand his journey in terms of the religious traditions of earlier days. For him it was simply a psychological fact. He understood the overt aspects of his journey in a quite casual and literalistic way. To him it was nothing more than a psychological technique that required him to close his eyes and concentrate on an inward flow of sounds and imagery, describing them as they came. All he did was let himself move freely in harmony with the psychological flow within him and undertake to be an honest reporter of what transpired.

In the course of his imaging, however, something changed in Carl's appreciation of what he was doing. The act of inward attention itself became filled with extraordinary significance, reflecting some of the intensity supplied by the image of the eyes in the statue and the open spaces in the stone. As a modern man, Carl did not possess any traditional symbols that could impart a quality of holiness to his experience; *but his psyche produced its own symbols out of its own need and out of its own wisdom.* These symbols had neither a traditional nor a ritualistic background, but their force and their validity were evident. They possessed the power to draw Carl as a modern man having no connection with any traditional doctrine to a firm experience of the spirituality inherent in the universe and his own close connection with it. The natural process of the psyche brought forth the necessary symbols and used them as vehicles to carry Carl to the point of a transforming contact within himself and to an awareness of transpersonal love.

The place where Carl made contact with meaning

and resource in his life was the place that has always
been the sacred place for man throughout all history,
the depths of his psyche. Now that Carl knew that one
enters another dimension of being, through the psyche,
he was glad to have access to it.

"This is quite a step that I have made," he told me.
"I feel that this is something constant, that it is always
in me and that it is always available to me. I felt this also
when I first discovered the contact, and now I realize
that it is a matter of being able to relax sufficiently to
have it."

What does "relaxing" mean in this context? It means
relaxing the bars of self-consciousness sufficiently to
permit the flow of imagery to move freely in the psyche.
It means being able to watch what takes place and report it honestly. It means becoming accustomed enough
to the style and the rhythms of the flow of imagery in
the psyche so that one feels at home when one goes
there. It means being at ease with the depths of the psyche, being able to go there from time to time for the
special knowledge and support it contains, and then returning to the world for outer expression.

The experience of contact gave Carl a sense of meaning and connection in his life. This was of great personal importance to him, but in a general way. Of what
specific benefit was it to him?

The major importance of his new contact with the
depth of his psyche was that Carl now had an inner
perspective with which to approach his daily life. This

was not an outer perspective in the sense of a conscious philosophy or a framework of ideas *about* life; it was a perspective that had been inwardly experienced and was effective as a new sensitivity to the inward dimension of things. Where Carl had felt alone in his life, he now felt connected. Again in this it was not an outward connection with people that was enlarged, but an inward connection with life. Carl derived from this the strength to endure the pain of certain frustrations which had to come before a new trend of fulfillment in his practical affairs would be possible.

Carl's main problem in classical psychological terms was his inferiority complex. He had always felt that others were better than he, that they were more capable, gifted with greater strength and abilities than he. Feeling this, he had been inhibited in expressing himself and he had been bothered by anxieties, fearing that he would not be able to succeed in the business world.

It is possible to analyze problems like these down to their earliest so-called cause in infancy, and still not make a dent in them. Very often, in fact, the more we analyze them, the more we tie ourselves to them, the tighter the symptoms become, and the more difficult it is to free ourselves. The alternative to the analytical way in psychotherapy is to work to stimulate the depth of the psyche until it brings forth symbolic contents that make possible a vital new experience of meaning in the individual's life.

When a new meaning is felt as a living experience

that validates itself by its power and presence in the individual's existence, a new center has been established for the personality as a whole. The entire range of individual activities then is altered; indeed, it alters itself. The person finds then that he is approaching his daily tasks with a new outlook so that, without even being conscious of what he is doing, he is creating a new life for himself. This is why the most effective and most direct way to heal psychological symptoms is to take the apparently circuitous route of going around them. They may be bypassed so that one can concentrate more fully on reaching a point of contact that will open a sensitivity to symbolic reality in the depth of the psyche derived from the individual's own inherent imagery.

Once this point of contact is touched and a new relation to the core and meaning of life is established, a new structure of personality comes into being, not deliberately but spontaneously, based upon an awareness of meaningful existence. The individual finds himself drawn, even dedicated, to work toward goals which have the effect of strengthening the momentum of the vital thrust in his personality. When a basic meaning of life is experienced deeply and symbolically as part of the spiritual growth of a person, there is no time for symptoms. They disappear for lack of attention and because they are out of place.

In Carl's situation, having made his contact, he felt a realization of a power that was present and accessible within him, available as a source of capacity whenever it would be needed. He knew that he now possessed the capacity to reach into the depth of himself for guidance and strength. He could do it in times of special need, and he could do it from time to time to enlarge his contact with his inner resources.

This sense of knowing the nature of the psychological resources upon which he could call if necessary was deeply reassuring to him. It went a long way toward eliminating the anxieties that had beset him from time to time, and had plagued him especially at crucial moments in his life. The feeling of being connected to life went a long way toward anticipating his anxieties and making them irrelevant. Carl did not need to be anxious now that he had actually experienced a contact with the symbolic, spiritually supportive dimension of existence. Further, now that he had entered the dimension of life on which people are joined together rather than separated as individuals, the feelings of competitiveness and the fears of failure because of his inferiority feelings now could be neutralized. He could now relate to people with openness and love, not because he believed in it intellectually and was in favor of good social relations, but because the contact that had happened to him manifested itself in a quality that drew other people to him. They felt his connection to life and to them, and they responded to it.

For all this, difficult situations would arise from time to time. It would, in particular, take some time to overcome business problems which his past attitudes had left as their legacy; but his contact would sustain him and would enable him to bear with his difficulties until the outer situation changed. Also, inevitably, with time he would lose the intensity of his contact and need to reestablish it. From time to time he would fall into depression and anxiety again, and he would have to struggle back up, as Tolstoy did, "once, twice, ten, a hundred times." But Carl now possessed the tools with which to make the journey again as many times as would be necessary. He had been there once, and he knew the way. He would grow with each new journey. He now felt strong psychologically because he knew that he had touched a spiritual source within himself that was valid not only for his own life but for all.

MR. HART EXTENDS A DREAM

A good example of how a modern person can work by himself to cultivate the process of the deep psyche was described in one of my New York seminar/workshops. These workshops consist of groups of approximately twenty persons who meet weekly to participate in a joint group experience. The content of these workshops varies, but they combine essentially two kinds of material: a discussion of insights and concepts drawn from depth psychology; and an amplification of these with individual experiences drawn from the group. The at-

tempt of those participating is to enter into these experiences and extend them from the inside as we share
them, thus enlarging the sensitivity of all in the group
to the dimension of symbolic reality.

At one workshop session a dream followed by an imaging experience was described by a member of the
group, Mr. Hart, a businessman in his fiftieth year. Mr.
Hart is an active executive with major responsibilities in
his private life; but he had also made the commitment
to himself to work in the symbolic process in order to
find new meaning and new channels of activity for the
later years of his life. It was in this context that he was
taking part in the workshop.

The dream which Mr. Hart told the group was a short
one. In it he found himself in front of a door which was
locked. It was a large door that seemed to be made of
heavy wood. On one side of the door there was a large
lock, and on the other side there were strong and impressive hinges. In the dream Mr. Hart found himself
trying to open the door in order to go through the door-
way, but he was not able to do so. He had no key. He
could not open the lock, but he kept trying to open the
door nevertheless. He tried to shove it open, to push it,
to pry it, using force in whatever way he could; but it
was all to no avail. All he succeeded in doing was to
bruise himself, and he felt the physical pain as well as
the frustration in the dream.

That was as far as the dream went. It brought him to

the door, gave him the desire to open it and pass through, and left him there stranded without recourse. It did indeed seem to lead to a dead end.

What is a person to do with a dream that draws him on and then closes as though it were springing a trap? Should he interpret it as a verdict which the psyche is rendering regarding his life? Does it mean that his existence has become a closed door with no means of passage? He will come to such a conclusion only if he approaches the dream intellectually and tries to read it from an analytical point of view. If he understands, however, that the dream is only a brief excerpt drawn from the ongoing flow in the depths of the psyche, he will know that he needs to draw no conclusion at all. No conclusion is called for because the psychic flow is still in motion. There is much more depth material to be drawn from the same place from which the dream came. Having told him this much regarding the closed door in his life, the psyche has much more to say. It is necessary, however, that he gain access to it; and the frustration of the dream was that it stopped before it had given a complete message.

Mr. Hart's task, then, was to get the dream started again so that he could find out what else was at work in the depths of his psyche. Obviously the dream itself was over; he had awakened from it, and he could not go back to sleep deliberately to dream that dream again. What he could do, however, was to sit back quietly and let himself feel the atmosphere of the dream until, in a twilight state between sleep and waking, the imagery of the dream would continue itself. He sat quietly and looked inward, his eyes closed, prepared to see the images upon the screen before the mind's eye if they would come.

He was following an aspect of the procedure which we described in the sessions with Carl, dropping down into the psyche in order to let the flow of imagery resume the action which had appeared in the dream. On three separate occasions after the dream, Mr. Hart tried this procedure without success. Nothing would come. He had been so impressed, however, by the strong emotional tone which the dream carried that he felt convinced it had something more to say to him. He therefore persisted, tried a fourth time, and this time succeeded. The dream imagery extended itself and led him along in a way he could not have foreseen.

"I felt that I was walking down a large lighted hallway," Mr. Hart told the group in describing the imagery that came to him.* "It was quite immense. I was not conscious of walking. Spaced evenly on both sides of this long hallway there was a series of doors, each of which was locked. I said to myself, 'Why am I here?' With that I took a deep breath and suddenly I smelled something that attracted me. As I breathed this odor it sort of magnetized me and I thought I have to get at the

* All direct quotations are taken from the tape recording of the seminar/workshop session.

source of it. I didn't really walk but just moved along the hallway until I came to this door, one particular door at the end of the hallway. I said, 'That smell is behind the door and I must get through.' Then came the dream in which I was struggling to get through the door."

It was only after the imagery had proceeded this far that Mr. Hart was brought back to the brief dream that had made so strong an impression on him. Now the atmosphere of that frustrating situation reappeared. He was once again before that large heavy door with its lock on one side and the hinges on the other. Once again he was trying to open it, pushing it at the side where it seemed that it might be opened, but with no success. He was straining there, struggling to get the door open, pushing at it, pulling at it, tugging at the left side where the lock was, then at the right side where the hinges were, all to no avail. Suddenly he had a feeling that someone was behind him, a shadowy, nonphysical person whose arms reached upward and around him, coming upward from the ground, reaching over his head, and easily pushing the door open in front of him *in the center*. Mr. Hart had been straining to open it at the sides where the lock and hinges were; but it had been opened for him in the center.

"And I just went in," Mr. Hart concluded his account. "I didn't know who did it, but I felt that it was someone who was very friendly to me. He was behind me and I didn't see him. I just knew he had done this. He had come up from behind me, had gone around my shoulders and over my head with his arms, and he had opened the door in front of me easily. He had just touched it and it had opened in the center like a swinging door. Then I went in and sort of merged into things on the other side. I just disappeared into the odor. And that was the story."

When Mr. Hart finished, the group began to discuss his experience. It was a movement of imagery with which they could easily identify. They felt the frustration of his dream and they noted how the extension of the material moved past the blockage on the symbolic level. A most striking effect of the experience was the change in attitude with which Mr. Hart emerged from it. He had entered it feeling stymied, since a heavy door which he could not open was barring his progress. The movement of the imagery, however, led him to feel that a friendly power was active in his life and was available to guide and sustain him.

The group remarked about the intensity with which Mr. Hart had strained to overcome the blockage of the locked door, both in the dream and in the imagery. When he found that he could not open the door because he did not have the key to it, he tried to break through by force. It was an attitude he had displayed before in his life when things he sought did not open easily to him. At this time too, he had large, though still undefined, goals for the next years of his life; and it was especially frustrating to him to realize that he did not have the key to them.

He would try to force the issue, using whatever means or strategem he could; but whatever he would try to do would be of no use. He himself would not be able to make the breakthrough. This was paralleled on the symbolic level by the deepening of the frustration as he walked along the hallway of locked doors in his imagery. He was seeking something there. What was it? He did not know, but he was being drawn on toward it nonetheless. He was following the scent of something, he knew not what. That was the role the special odor played in the imaging. It was drawing him on as though by a magnetic attraction; and another way to phrase that would be to say that it was guiding him.

Not by his own conscious powers but by something of whose nature he was not aware, the way was being shown to him. He could proceed just by sniffing it out, that is, in an elemental way, nonrationally, intuitively. Finally when he reached the door he reverted to his old style; still not possessing the key himself, he tried to open the door by force. Not so though; he himself could not do it. But another power could. This other power, separate from himself, and yet somehow intimately connected with him, did it for him with ease and with knowledge. This spirit-like being was like a person, and yet was not a person. Mr. Hart said that there was something profoundly awesome in the experience, and the members of the group saw this in his bearing as he spoke of it. We felt it as a fact among us all.

Curiously, no one in the group spoke of it as God. Perhaps that was because no one needed to.

MRS. WHITE'S TWILIGHT IMAGERY

Mr. Hart's way of working involved the combination of group work with the personal extension of dream and imagery material at home alone. This method could have an affirmative effect for him because of his commitment to keeping an honest record and to refrain from interpreting his symbolic material in an analytical way. He had a feeling for the reality of the inward flow in terms of the principle of symbolic unfoldment; and this validated itself for him still further in the experience we have just described. He possessed the capacity to bear with it and to draw it along, to walk along the hallway of locked doors, until the answer came within its own terms, not intellectually, but on the level of intuition and imagery where its power could be both known and expressed.

On a parallel path, Mrs. White followed the same commitment to recording the events of the inner life. Unlike Mr. Hart, however, she combined this with regular person-to-person consultations in a continuing dialogue relationship. She utilized the twilight imaging procedure as one of her methods of drawing forward the movement of her psychic life as a whole. It was part of a large program of personal growth which included the sensitive observance of her dreams and imagery, maintaining a continuing record of her experiences in a psychological workbook, drawing them forward by going into the deep flow of the psyche both at home alone and in the dialogue relationship which we had established, and using this relationship to provide an inward perspective of growth with which to keep a balance through the cycles of emotion and conflict in her environmental life.

The cumulative effect of this work was a much larger personal vista and a change in her conception of what is real in life to a degree that can conservatively be called a spiritual transformation. It involved her reawakening to the potentialities of life at the point where her children reached mid-teens and it included certain personal problems which were a residue of the earlier years. All of the personal aspects of her life, however, were encompassed by the new quality of awareness carried by her symbolic experiences. These brought her level of consciousness to a dimension where the difficult personal situations could be absorbed, and they opened resources of energy and insight that demonstrated again the transformative power of the deep psyche.

Of the several significant experiences which occurred at different stages of the work, one is of particular interest in our present context. This experience also began, as did Mr. Hart's, with a brief fragment of a dream that carried a great intensity of feeling with it. It may be that such brief dreams present a more definite impression of having left their work unfinished; and thus the movement of imagery connected with them is more readily begun anew.

The dream possessed a heavy and serious atmosphere. "I felt," Mrs. White told me, "as if I were watching a Greek tragedy." There was a feeling of something very large involved in the action of the dream, something almost epic in scope, pertaining to the universals of human life. This was why the quality of Greek tragedy was felt to pervade it. Despite this, the actual content of the dream was very simple, modern in context, and with overtones of her personal life.

In the dream a man was returning to his home and as he did so a woman stepped forward from the house and said in exceedingly dramatic style, "All is different. I am blind now." That was all she could remember of the dream, except that a swimming pool seemed also to be part of the situation.

We did not discuss the dream in detail on the conscious level, but Mrs. White closed her eyes, turned her attention into the depths of herself, and quickly returned to the atmosphere of the dream. Once there, she was able to elaborate the feeling of what had transpired between the two people of the dream. For the woman to say, "I am blind now," Mrs. White explained to me, is like saying, "all is over." It is as if there is no use now, nothing further can be done. There is no use in his coming home. The imagery became active then and there was some discussion in it between the man and the woman. The man was confused and acted as though he were rather intimidated by the things the woman had said to him. For a moment it seemed as though the relationship between them was going to break apart completely.

At that point the movement of the imagery took another turn. The idea came to the woman then that things would get better if the two of them went swimming. She had the feeling that if they both dived into the pool her blindness would go away and she would be able to see again. The man, however, was reluctant. He didn't want to go swimming, and though she tried to persuade him, he remained adamant. He would not go into the water. Finally the woman dived into the pool alone and swam around by herself.

Mrs. White was now describing the images to me as they came before her mind's eye, and as she felt them. "The woman dives into the water now," she said, "and it feels very cool on her eyes. It feels very good. She swims way down to the bottom of the pool. She can see. She realizes that she can see under water. Her eyes feel very rested, very cool, very comforted. She feels good. She is swimming around at the bottom of the pool and she feels very cool and relaxed and comforted.

The tone of feeling now was soft and quiet, but the tempo and the intensity of the imaging increased. "The

woman is coming to the top of the pool now," Mr
White reported to me. "She finds that she can see. Sh
not only could see at the bottom of the water, but no
on the top as well. She can see outside, all around he
She finds that she can see everything; and it is differe
now. Everything is very light and brilliant. The air
just full of sunlight. It is dancing with sunlight." The
was an exhilaration in Mrs. White's voice as she t
me this.

She continued. "She can see farther than she e
could see before. And much, much more clearly. Eve
thing is sharply etched as though it were up close e
though it is far away. She can see mountains in the
tance. They are very far, but she can see them
sharply as though they were up close. She can see t
mountains farther and clearer than she ever could
fore. She can see the tall trees on these mountains
can see the rocks on the mountaintop, and she ca
bits of snow—even small bits of snow—very clearl

There was a brief pause, as though Mrs. White w
countering something new or additional on the im
level. She went on. "She is looking at people. Sh
see people in a special way. She can look at peop
see way behind their eyes." There was a tone of a
ment, of quiet awe, in Mrs. White's voice as sh
this; but she went on without interruption.

"She can look in back of their eyes, and she
things that their eyes are hiding, or things th

don't even know." There was another pause, as though a further perception was appearing that was even more strange to her.

"She looks down at the ground and she can see even way into the earth. She can look down and see the ants in the earth moving round, and she can see the worms crawling round underneath the ground. She looks further into the ground, deeper, way beneath the surface, and she sees things. She sees beneath the rocky ledge under the earth. She sees a stream of water moving under it. It is strong, a great stream of water under the earth, and now she sees wells coming up from it."

A tremendous intensity was in the room by this time. Mrs. White was indeed feeling that a special quality of vision had come to her, bringing with it a contact with a resource hidden in the depths of things. She felt the power of it becoming accessible to her. It was expressed in the fullness of feeling that accompanied the imagery, especially in the latter part of it. The image of the wells through which the deep subsurface waters were tapped carried this sense of linkage, connecting the power of the depths with the surface of life.

At this point in the imagery I called "time," judging that we had reached a good point to rest and to consider what had taken place. I also asked Mrs. White to write down when she left the office as much of the imagery experience as she could retain. She was accustomed to do this, and she was usually able to make an accurate and full report which accorded quite well with

my notes and tape recording. This time, however, when she went to make her description of the experience it would not come out in its usual form. The tone of what had transpired was apparently too intense for prose. It seemed that the experience "wanted" to describe itself in the form of poetry; and Mrs. White had come far enough in our work to be able to let it have its way. She was not given to versifying, but the following lines are the version of the experience which Mrs. White brought to me a few days later.

I told the man "I am blind. You have come too late."
But I entered the pool and opened my eyes
I saw a stone and a tree on the farthest peak;
I saw the stars in the sky in the daytime;
I saw under the soil: the ants and the worms,
    The rock ledge and the rivers of water;
And I saw behind the man's eyes;
    Behind the lies and the ignorance,
    I saw a butterfly—
And I said, "It is not too late."

OPEN VISION AND LOVE

It was apparent when Mrs. White read the poem to me that the last lines referred to something that had not been part of the imaging she had done in the office. How had she happened to add them?

She described what had taken place. When she had gotten ready to write her imaging experience, the intensity of what she had felt immediately returned to her with full force. She found that she could not proceed to tell the story of the imagery events in her direct reporting style; it seemed to phrase itself as poetry. It was perhaps more the mood than the form of poetry, and the mood of the imaging took over once again. She found herself deep in the symbol, and as she began to write about it the symbol began to unfold as it had before.

Once again she found herself to be blind, and then she was diving into the swimming pool. It was hardly necessary to point out to her how spontaneously she had identified herself with the woman in the dream. She felt her blindness, and she felt it disappear as she went down into the water. During this second experience of the symbol, she told me, it had become clear to her that the diving into the pool was the equivalent of her going down into the depths of her psyche. It was saying to her that when she lived on the surface of things she was as one who is blind; but when she went into the dimension of depth, her eyes opened and she could see. She could see in the depths, but more important, when she returned to the outward side of life her vision could still penetrate beneath the surface of things. This was not larger intellectual understanding; it was vision that reached beneath the surface of things and people because it proceeded directly from the depths of the psyche. It carried with it a sensation of "opening" of vision, not so much the capacity of outward vision as inward cognitive vision. It carried a quality of feeling that was new for her and that enlarged the scope of her perception. It seemed to give her access to another dimension of reality, as though the intensity of awareness on the imagery level of the psyche involved a style of sight that penetrated the opaque surfaces of the outer world.

I saw the stars in the sky in the daytime;
I saw under the soil: the ants and the worms,
　The rock ledge and the rivers of water;

The very act of writing intensified the capacity of open vision, which had suddenly become real to her. The symbol then continued to unfold out of its own momentum. It went on and carried her sensitivity of vision beyond objects in nature, beyond the stars, the soil, the rocks, the rivers. Now her capacity to see into the depths applied also to a human being, to the man who had been in the dream and who had been adamant toward the woman in the imagery.

As the symbol extended itself, her feeling toward the man softened. Her vision entered him, reached "behind the man's eyes," into the core of him, into the seed of reality in him "behind the lies and the ignorance" clouding the surface. Seeing behind the man's eyes did not mean that she looked more sharply and analytically through his motivations to diagnose his weaknesses; it meant rather that she saw through the inadequate façades of his life to the reality in him that had been vainly trying to come to expression. She could see through to the seed of personality in the man, what had remained latent in him and undeveloped through all the years she had known him. She perceived the potential in him as a person, and she felt it as real even though it had never fulfilled itself in life. She saw it as real enough to touch, to hold, and to affirm with an encompassing feeling that warmed the total situation in the depth of herself.

In contrast to this, the attitude pervading the dream and the beginnings of the imagery indicated that the man was being held in judgment. It seemed that the woman was implicitly judging him and that it was this act of judgment that had drawn the situation to an impasse. It carried a tone of finality, as though a verdict had been cast. It deprived the relationship of the fluidity that was necessary if new elements were to enter it and alter it. Perhaps it was this psychological rigidity that had given the overtone of Greek tragedy to the dream.

It is interesting to note that even in the brief dream fragment there was the implication that her act of judgment was superficial and that her blindness was related to the quality of her judgment. The imagery moved spontaneously in the direction of overcoming this. As it progressed, the nature of the vision that pierced beneath the surface into the heart of things gave Mrs. White a perspective that went beyond judgment. This vision did not see things as they are on the surface, fixed in a mold; but it saw the principle of growth working underneath. It saw the possibility in the person, a possibility that was still open and was therefore too young to be judged, not matter how old in years and how world-weary the person in whom it was working. Feeling this principle at work, to judge the man became irrelevant.

The image that accompanied this change in the consciousness of Mrs. White was a butterfly. The two came together, the change in the quality of consciousness and the image with which it was dramatized. It is not that one preceded or "caused" the other, but that each accompanied the other, for there is much evidence to indicate that the psyche moves in terms of "correspondences." The butterfly is a natural embodiment of new and delicate transformation, and it was therefore an apt representation of the newly emergent capacity in the psyche. The flow of imagery in the writing of the poem gave the new attitude its expression:

I saw a butterfly—
And I said, "It is not too late."

With this, the process of symbolic unfoldment had carried the situation around full circle. Her original attitude was reversed because her perception of existence was now established in terms of the depth dimension of life which she had experienced, as only it can be experienced, upon the depth level of the psyche. Where her relationship to the man had been hardening because the avenues of change had been closed off by negative judgments, the way of growth, which could become growth toward each other, was opened again. She no longer judged in terms of outer appearances, but directed her attention to the reality unfolding in the depth of the man. Thus she did not need to judge at all, but only to affirm and to wait.

We must ask, however, how *real* this that Mr. White saw could be. It referred to something in the man that had not shown itself before; at least, she had not seen it. How *real* then could it be? It was as real as a seed in the earth that is trying to grow though it is covered by a stone. If she saw only the stone, that would be the end of it. But if she could see through the stone to perceive the seed behind it, she would be able to free the seed and enable it to grow.

The analogy of the seed is apt, but it has a serious drawback. Unfortunately, the seed of potentiality in a human being is not nearly so tangible as the seed of a flower. We can perceive a seed that lies in the ground. We can water it, fertilize it, and care for it until it matures. But how can we perceive the seed in other human beings when their surface attitude is hard and opaque and often antagonistic, as though it were designed specifically to prove that no seed is there.

Mrs. White's imagery indicates the answer to this. Her dream began with just such a feeling. It was expressed in her blindness. She could not see the seed in the man. But then she dived into the pool, into the depths of the psyche, and there she reached an intense awareness of the dimension of reality that lies beneath the surface of things. The capacity to *see the seed through the stone* was given to her by means of her participation in the process of symbolic unfoldment. This did not involve a doctrine, not a belief nor an idea that a person can agree with or be in favor of. It was a fact of experience, something that happened to her. When it had happened to her, her capacity of awareness became different from what it had been before. She could *see* differently. She could see through the surface to the reality behind it; and this new capacity of perception was what enabled her to perceive the seed in the man and to overcome her negative judgments of him, even though the outward evidence was all to the contrary.

Even then, her perception of the seed in him was nothing definite. It was only a feeling of connection and a receptivity to the seed in another person. She could not say specifically what his seed was. But this is one of the things that love is called upon to do: To affirm and sustain the seed in a fellow human being even though no tangible evidence has been given of the nature and quality of the seed that is growing there. Love is needed while the seed is still a potentiality. After it has come forth, the support of love is not nearly so necessary; praise and encouragement are sufficient then.

In this sense, the capacity to love depends upon the capacity to feel the reality of the future before it has tipped its hand, before the seed has disclosed itself, and while there is still no more specific basis for judgment than a feeling that links the depths of one person to the seed in the depths of another. Love depends upon the capacity to reach beneath the surface of persons, to feel and touch the seed of life that is hidden there. And love becomes a power when it is capable of evoking that seed and drawing it forth from its hiding place.

To be philosophically in favor of the power of evocative love does not, unfortunately, make it come to pass. Not even to be by temperament a so-called "loving person" will make it possible. It requires a direct encounter with the symbolic dimension of reality to awaken the capacity of open perception at the depth level of the psyche. Then love as an active, evocative power becomes possible. There are many exhortations in favor of love, and many simple formulae have been espoused for the techniques of loving; but there is no substitute for the commitment to disciplined work in the depth of oneself. Creative love becomes psychologically possible when the work of sensitizing the depths of personality has been carried through.

This work is sometimes a slow process, and sometimes it moves by leaps and bounds. It gathers momentum after a while, and by this is sometimes carried forward by giant strides. But it is often indistinct at the beginning, or at least until a first experience of contact has transpired. Primarily it depends upon an act of dedication that is inwardly verified. It is an act of loyalty to oneself that is validated moment by moment as one feels a growing capacity to recognize reality in its symbolic dimension; and as one finds oneself increasingly translating this awareness into acts of love.

Mrs. White is an instance of a modern person who made this commitment, both out of need and out of desire. The experience which we discussed, culminating in symbolic unfoldment in the form of a poem, is one of several that opened spiritual vistas for her in psychological terms. There are many lessons we can draw from it, but one in particular is worth investigating now. It is the principle, which Mrs. White's psychological work exemplifies, that the basic step in solving personal psychological problems is to avoid attacking them head-on. The best progress is made indirectly, by shifting the attention away from the specific problem or symptom, to the depth level of the psyche. There, by permitting the elemental symbol to unfold, a new quality of awareness is achieved by which the original problem is placed in a new perspective that restructures it so that it can be resolved. This important insight and contribution of depth psychology was visible in the work done with each of the persons whom we have discussed. It has large implications because of the personal therapeutic results it brings to the individual, especially since its therapeutic effect is achieved by opening the way for a deep and convincing experience of meaning in life. It has an importance, however, that is even greater than the personal results it brings. The fact that it makes possible for individuals a steadily enlarging symbolic recognition of ultimate aspects of human existence has great social implications as well. By means of such procedures many persons may become capable of entering the symbolic realm of human experience, learning to feel at home with it, thus gaining access to the larger dimensions of reality which the modern personality requires. It is this possibility that we should now explore to see what type of program may be followed to enable us to meet the human problem of our time at its fundamental levels.

5 A program for personal growth

THE MAKING OF AN ATMOSPHERE

One of the major problems of living in a period of history such as ours, which is a late and declining point in a civilization, is the weakness in its structure of symbols. The power has gone out of old beliefs, and they are no longer capable of providing a framework of meaning for the lives of many persons. This is simply a historical fact related to the historical circumstances in which we live. We have to recognize this fact before we can answer the further question of how symbols can be made strong when history has made them weak.

For a great many persons in modern times the traditional symbols of previous generations have become hollow. They no longer contain beliefs that can be felt to be sacred realities of life. But here we have the key to the problem. The weakness of the specific symbols is not the heart of the difficulty. Where certain symbols lose their force as beliefs others can easily be substituted for them. During the period of Old Testament history when the nature of ritual observance altered and when many fundamental beliefs changed, beliefs about the individual's relation to God, immortality, and the Messiah, the underlying conception of spiritual reality remained firm. Particular beliefs changed, but the encompassing feeling for what is ultimately real remained in the background as a sustaining atmosphere. Similarly, during the generations of active change in modern Christian doctrine which brought the various Protestant sects into being, there was a tremendous ferment which saw the rejection and radical alteration of many traditional symbols. But the underlying context of these beliefs remained strong. In fact, the intensity of the struggles during the years of the Reformation were an indication of how deeply the Christian conception of life was experienced by the European community as a whole. It was a sustaining atmosphere of feeling that pervaded the minds of men at the deepest levels so that while they were arguing about beliefs on the surface level of doctrine, they were implicitly in deeper agreement as to the dimensions of what they inwardly experienced, and assumed, reality to be.

Within such a framework of underlying assumptions as to the nature of reality—whatever its specific conceptions may be—a civilization can endure its struggles and transformations. It can emerge even stronger than it began, but its inner conviction of what is ultimately real in life must be so conclusively felt that it does not need to be thought about. Then it will not be shaken by changes in doctrinal belief, but it will serve as the psychological atmosphere in which individuals in the civilization can move about and have their being. Whether or not it is based upon "true" conceptions of the nature of life, they are able to conduct their lives within its contexts and definitions. But if there is no such atmosphere of abiding knowledge, or if there is so great a turmoil and flux on this fundamental level of cultural life that no one framework of belief can be experienced by individuals, a vacuum is set up where a sustaining atmosphere should be.

This becomes a primary social fact when it occurs. The lack of inner support is felt in the background of the culture as a whole, but it is experienced most intensely within the individual. With no sustaining atmosphere, he has no basis for self-orientation and no means of finding a meaning in his life. This is the core of the experience of meaninglessness that has led to the psychological inabilities of modern man.

It is true that even in addition to the Biblical and Christian context of reality, there are several other sets of symbolic belief available to modern persons. These may take the form of special religious doctrines, Eastern or Western in origin, or secular faiths and ideologies of many kinds. But each of these presents a special version of truth made to measure for a particular predisposition. They seem not to be adequate for a world which has been shown, both by science and by the dangers of history, a vision of truth beyond provincial opinions. To carry out the work of reconstructing persons, modern man requires a new context of belief based upon a symbol so elemental that it touches the depth beyond all subjectivity, and so encompassing that it gives meaning to all without rejecting any.

A symbol of that scope cannot be constructed deliberately by an act of intellect. It requires the support of a profound and continuing experience. It involves not a set of beliefs consciously held but an *atmosphere*, a quality of *feeling* about the nature of reality. To state, for example, that the psyche is the directive principle of the human being by which man touches the universe and discovers the ever-enlarging meaning of his existence, is in itself only a descriptive statement. To conceive of the psyche and to describe it is an act of intellect. To this degree it is an act of partial being; but to involve oneself in the cycles and struggles by which the meanings of human existence unfold through the psyche, is an act of total being. It is an act of participation in the wholeness of life, and by means of it the individual enters a larger dimension of reality.

In the accumulation of acts of this type, as numerous persons individually enlarge the dimensions of their experience, a special atmosphere of reality comes into the world. Person by person, the relation to life alters and introduces a new depth of meaningfulness. This is how a culture changes its structure of values and belief. Not by authority of doctrine, but by the progressive deepening of experiences of involvement in life, a new substrate of belief forms itself, person by person.

The transformation of the mentality that constitutes the basic tone of a culture is a large, generalized, and gradual process. Its components, however, are personal experiences; and in this sense the establishment of a new relation to reality in a civilization is specifically composed of the experiences of individuals. The encounters in the psyche which we have described are such building blocks by which a new structure of beliefs about reality can be brought into being.

When a person struggles in the depths of his psyche, gradually drawing forth a larger relation to truth out of his repeated cycles of depression, the quality of the experience itself becomes a fact of the world. In a certain way it becomes an awareness that belongs to all. As though it were part of a group experience, it becomes a factor in the psyche of the community as a whole.

This is true not only of the great spiritual figures— men like Dostoyevsky and Herman Hesse, Einstein and

Tagore and Gandhi—who have recorded their experiences or lived them in public, and whose articulateness has enabled them to communicate at least an indication of the events that transpired within them. It is true as well of more humble individuals whose encounters in the psyche can never be more than privately known. It was true of Carl, of whom we have spoken, as he entered the realm of spaceless space and learned to participate in a dimension of spiritual reality that was quite in accord with modern science. It was true of Mr. Hart as he went down the hallway of closed doors following an inward scent until an unexpected guidance came to him. The matter-of-fact reality he had known in the business world was then transcended by his awareness of a greater and more fundamental dimension of reality. It was true of Mrs. White as she dived into the depths of her imagery and emerged with a quality of knowledge that made the capacity to love tangible and real to her.

For each of these persons, the expansion of their relation to reality was not an isolated event in their lives. It was part of a continuing commitment which involved a steady enlargement of their sensitivity to the inward dimension of existence. It included an awareness of the cycles of the psyche, of the dynamics of imagery, and of the principles by which elemental symbols unfold within a person until they establish a connection to life of transpersonal magnitude. It involved, most fundamentally, a conception of the nature of human existence

conceived not as an intellectual theory but as a participation in reality. It was a living experience for them,
implemented by a regular and disciplined practice de-
voted to evoking and cultivating the faculties of the
psyche.

In each of these individuals, the conception of human
existence and the psychological disciplines practiced to
fulfill it led to a greater wholeness of personal being.
They enlarged the experience of meaning in life. In addition to this, when taken collectively, they comprise a
social point of view, a symbolic attitude toward life
comparable to the substrate of belief which we have
seen to be a necessity for modern civilization if modern
man is to develop a methodology for spiritual growth
equal to his needs.

The key to such a transformation would seem to be a
new symbol strong enough to redirect the energies of
personality. But how shall we choose such a symbol?
Which symbol shall we call upon and how shall we make
it effective? By the nature of the task it is called upon to
fulfill, such a symbol would depend upon the quality of
awareness which each individual validates for himself
in the privacy of his own experience. No specific symbol
can meet this need. It is rather that the process itself,
the encompassing process by which inward reality unfolds on the dimension of depth of the psyche, is itself
the symbol that can serve *operationally* to meet the
modern need for spiritual transformation achieved by
psychological means.

The experience of this process is personal, but taken collectively and cumulatively it becomes a socially shared perception of reality which enables a new quality of feeling to permeate the culture as a whole through the increasing and deepening experience of individuals. At first these experiences seem to be subjective, and the individuals to whom they come are hesitant and apologetic about them. As they continue and increase, however, the very quality of their subjectivity becomes an objective context of communication. It then becomes possible for individual and group experiences to reinforce one another so that the new conception of reality increasingly permeates the thought and feeling of the community. In this way, over a period of time, a social and personal atmosphere is established in which the depth dimension is increasingly felt to be the context of reality.

Reflecting on the experience of Carl, Mr. Hart, and Mrs. White, we can realize how it is possible for such an atmosphere to be brought into being, person by person. The psychological essence of the procedures which these individuals followed was expressed in the subtle change that took place in the focus of attention, shifting it away from outward concerns in a way that gave priority to an inward principle. This principle was not subject to their conscious manipulation, and it was not directed toward satisfying their ego desires. It followed its own nature, and worked to fulfill its own requirements.

The essence of the method used in each case was the recognition of the integrity with which the inward principle unfolds. Special care was taken to give it all the freedom it needed to express its autonomy and to establish a new situation in the life of the individual. This meant placing the focus of consciousness at the depth level of the psyche and permitting the elemental symbols at work there to reshape the structure of the personality in accordance with their inner form and rhythm.

In this procedure the individual turns aside from the anxieties and interests of the moment and directs his attention to the inward process of symbolic unfoldment. He does not attempt to direct the movement of the symbolic principle at work, but rather takes an open and permissive attitude toward it. Within the depths of the psyche he permits it to direct him, as Mr. Hart, for example, held his ego in check and followed the scent down the hallway. He thus placed himself in a position to be surprised by a new source of guidance appearing unexpectedly from within. The attitude underlying this is the key to the methodology of personal growth.

How shall such a process be initiated? It seems that modern man cannot depend on external supports or cultural directives. Because of the intense individuality to which he has developed, and because of his special historical circumstances, whatever he is to accomplish in his personal development he will have to achieve by himself as an individual. The development of a deep capacity of awareness in the modern individual is thus the precondition for any significant change that may be brought about in our civilization. It involves an underlying awareness on the part of persons, and it requires a continuing and deepening experience to support it. Establishment of this quality of mind and spirit in numerous modern individuals is the essence of the social atmosphere that is necessary if acts of personal transformation are to take place in our time.

This atmosphere does not depend upon any special doctrine of belief. Deliberate statements of faith are not part of it, and yet intense involvement and personal commitment play an important role in it. Primarily this atmosphere does not express a doctrine consciously held but a quality of feeling which is, at its core, a sense of being intimately related to the unfolding depths of being; it is an attitude of sensitivity with respect to the symbolic dimension.

As an atmosphere, it is intangible; and because of this, it requires definite disciplines to open the way for it, to sustain it, and to give it specific form. Here depth psychology is a valuable source. Its experience in healing neurosis by working toward the wholeness of persons has led to a variety of practical procedures. These provide a perspective in which we can chart a program of personal disciplines by which to establish a new atmosphere of inward reality.

Such a program has three main components:

1. Regular face-to-face consultations in a dialogue relationship to explore and evoke the individuality of the psyche.
2. The maintenance of a psychological workbook in which to keep a continuing record of all the varied contents and encounters on the depth level of experience.
3. Participation in group workshops in which experiences can be shared with other individuals who have embarked on the path of personal growth, and in which group techniques can be used by a competent leader for developing a greater sensitivity to the symbolic dimension.

These three aspects of a program for the development of persons reflect the different relationships in which the individual can carry on the work. The keeping of the workbook is done by the individual alone; the face-to-face consultations bring him into intimate dialogue with one other person; and the workshops involve him in the larger interaction of a group.

Ultimately all work of personal growth is a lonely endeavor. Always an individual is drawn into the search for meaning in life by an experience that is uniquely his. It may be a painful experience of confusion that starts him on the road; or it may be an intense inner calling to proceed in a direction the destination of which is not described. Not being described, it cannot be communicated; and it is thus that the main first phases of the search for meaning and the early development of the faculties of the spirit are carried on in an atmosphere of personal isolation. At that point, the nature of the experience cannot be shared, and this increases the intensity of the loneliness in which the search must be conducted. It makes it all the more essential that eventually a point of social contact be established so that the individual can be joined and supported as he passes through his aloneness to a larger connection to life.

DIALOGUE IN DEPTH

In this work, it is of crucial importance for an individual to establish a relationship with another human being with whom he can explore and stimulate his inner life. This does not refer to the spontaneous and intermittent meetings which strong friendship provides, valuable and enjoyable though those are. It refers, rather, to regular and disciplined meetings in a structured context where the pattern and direction of the individual's life can be examined objectively, interpreted, evaluated, and drawn forward. For this to be possible, a relationship of true dialogue must be established. The word, *dialogue,* here is to be understood in the large sense in which Martin Buber has used the term.* It does not refer to a congenial conversation between two persons, but to a meeting at a depth of being where a shared ex-

* See Martin Buber, *I and Thou.*

perience of the fundamentals of life draws two human beings together.

When this dialogue in depth is achieved, it has the effect of drawing the focus of attention steadily below the surface level of subjective personality, beyond the range of environmental concerns, to the depths of the elemental symbols. Here the potentials of the person are drawn forth in transpersonal terms that progressively restructure the capacities of knowledge and action.

The second person in the dialogue, the person who has the responsibility of acting as its director, finds himself fulfilling several roles. He acts as the balancer of the psyche as he stirs and harmonizes the tensions between the old patterns of the personality and the new quality of awareness seeking to emerge. He acts as the conductor and regulator of the psyche as he intuits by means of his own sensitivity the potentials of the person, and he maintains a perspective of this in the midst of the anxieties and overenthusiasms that occur in the course of the work. Most of all, however, he acts as an evoker of the images that are latent in the depth of the psyche, and he uses the principle of symbolic unfoldment to draw forth and establish the larger capacities and relation to life in the emergent person.

In achieving this, a variety of techniques and procedures are called upon. The continuity of dreams is worked with, the transient dreams that reflect everyday life and the lasting dreams of major import that are brought up from the deep foundations of human existence. A perspective of the inner development of the person is gradually put together so that the individual can feel not only the impediments of his past but the latent potentials striving toward fulfillment in his future. Gaining this perspective he can recognize and affirm the unborn possibilities of his life, and he can make room for their growth even while they are still invisible seeds. He can identify them from the shadows they cast ahead of themselves in the forms of dreams and imagery. To facilitate this, the procedure of *twilight imaging* is used to draw forth the flow of images from the kaleidoscope level of the psyche, and to find the forms, the patterns, and the symbolic meanings that the images wish to take.

Altogether the work of depth dialogue comprises a process of education in the largest sense of the term, a drawing forth of the spiritual wholeness implicit in human personality. As the work succeeds, it establishes in the person an intuitive knowing of the inner tempo and style of his psyche. He learns how to move with it, to roll with it, to rise and fall with it. He develops the capacity to enter the dimension of symbols and to deepen his experiences in terms of the nature of psychic reality. He gains a knowledge of how to withstand attacks of anxiety by utilizing the principles of the psyche; and by means of this knowledge, also, he learns to draw his personal existence into harmony with the elemental principles of life, as these principles are mirrored in the depth of the psyche.

It is significant to note that this relationship of depth dialogue has its prototype in the traditions of the major historical religions wherever disciplines for the development of individuals have been devised. Invariably, a period of structured work with a second person seems to be necessary, a person chosen for his authority and special competence. He may serve as a teacher charged with the task of inculcating a special doctrine or occult wisdom. He may act as a spiritual guide directing the development of the individual, as a guru, or a Zen master, or an Hasidic rabbi. Especially, he may also serve as an *evoker*, as Socrates did, using discourse as a means of arousing latent capacities of knowledge.

Curiously, however, the form in which the dialogue relationship has entered Western civilization is in the practice of psychiatry. It has been used most extensively in certain forms of psychotherapy stemming from psychoanalysis where it has provided a format for psychological healing in specifically medical terms. With the passage of time it has become increasingly apparent that even to meet the medical goal of psychological healing it is necessary to lead the individual to an experience of meaning that fulfills his individual nature. The second generation of psychoanalysts after Freud have found themselves steadily drawn into acting out a quasi-spiritual role, but without having tools of knowledge or techniques equal to the task. Now the extension of depth psychology to provide a program for the reclamation of personality in Western civilization enables us to establish the use of psychological tools in a large historical context to meet the cultural needs of our time. In this perspective, the conduct of depth dialogue as a means of evoking the spiritual wholeness of persons may evolve as the new style of psychological relationship expressing the life of the spirit in a scientific age.

PSYCHOLOGICAL WORKBOOKS

Once an individual has achieved an inner perspective of the psyche and has experienced the symbolic mode by which it acts as a reflector of reality, he is ready for further steps. The work of drawing forth the wholeness of personality can then be pursued in additional ways, especially by the regular keeping of a psychological workbook, and by active participation in group workshops whose focus is the sharing and extension of experiences in the psyche.

To maintain a psychological workbook for a significant period of time can be of major value in developing the capacities of personality. It must be understood, however, that a workbook is not simply a diary, nor is it a private journal. It is much more than a listing of events as they transpire in an individual's life; and it is much more also than a literary description, interpretation, and defense of the acts and attitudes one has taken in the course of the years. A psychological workbook is a continuing confrontation of oneself in the midst of life.

By means of it, a person can enter ever deeper into the meaning both of the external events of his life and his symbolic visions and dreams until he reaches the ground of reality upon which inward and outer experiences come together and join as two sides of a single coin.

Among the things that a psychological workbook should contain are a continuing record of dreams, described as they occur, and an account of events and associations that precede and surround them. The dreams should not be analyzed but only recorded and extended. The individual is not to interpret them but is to amplify them with his reflections and with such additional images as come to him in the course of recording and re-experiencing his dreams. In this way, the process by which individuality is seeking to unfold in the depths of the psyche is assisted in its integral development. It is then able to draw itself forward by its own style, and by its own rhythm generate a momentum that accords with its inherent pattern. Also as the continuity of dreams is recorded, the movement of the psyche is able to set its own context without being falsified by intellectual concepts. The ongoing flow of dreams and other imagery materials permits a framework of meaning to unfold from within its own contents. Meanings are thus not superimposed by a theory drawn from outside; they unfold from within the continuity of the dream record itself.

In the workbook all the relationships that are important in the individual's life can be set down, explored, and encountered anew. The mere act of careful and honest description made tangible by being written down is an important step in clarification. The gathering of insight occurs naturally and spontaneously, and it is cumulative as the work progresses. Most important, the act of making a written description of an experience serves itself to carry the process of the psyche forward. We saw, for example, that when Mrs. White was making her record of the sessions of *twilight imaging* she had had, her writing autonomously assumed the form of poetry. It then continued under its own power and brought forth an important addition to the original experience. This is a characteristic course of events when a person follows the workbook procedure. Not only in writing a description of an imagery experience that has already been a shared experience, but in recording a dream, or in writing an account of an event or relationship involving another person or a problem situation, the act of writing has a creative effect in drawing the position of the psyche further than it was before.

In this context we can see that the keeping of a psychological workbook possesses an active quality that makes it a dynamic tool to be used in evoking larger personal capacities. The act of writing stimulates the very psychic process that it is engaged in describing, and draws the process further ahead. The entries in the workbook are not a kind of personal journalism; they are not disengaged acts of reporting coolly written after the event. On the contrary, the writing of the workbook is an important part of the events themselves. Here again we can see that a psychological workbook is not at all to be compared to a personal diary. It is not a passive retelling of events that happened yesterday; and it is by no means self-conscious, analytical introspection. It is an active and continuing involvement in the inward process of the psyche by which an individual is drawn through his anxieties to a larger experience of reality in his personal existence.

In keeping his psychological workbook the person participates in the events of his life anew, recreating them and reopening them so that his relationships in life restructure themselves in the midst of the workbook. The act of writing the dream and of concerning oneself with its message becomes a reentering into the place of depth within oneself. In entering the atmosphere of a psychological workbook regularly, a person goes to the one place where the elusive flow of the psyche can be captured and made tangible. Thus, if the entries are made regularly over a sufficient period of time, significant insights become possible. One can mark off the variations in moods, the anxieties and depressions as compared to the times of exhilaration. Over a period of time the psychological workbook can be used to give the individual a feeling of his own psychic rhythms. With this as a source of empirical information concerning the subjective process working within him, he can gradually devise a means of correlating his inner tempo with his engagement in external events. When these two are brought into harmony, many of life's pressures ease and much more can be accomplished. Thus, when it is properly used, the psychological workbook can become the individual's own laboratory in which the trial-and-error experimenting of personal growth is recorded, studied, and grappled with until the goal of a transforming experience is reached.

We can see in this too that there is an important difference between keeping a psychological workbook and recording a spiritual journal. In most cases, a spiritual journal is essentially a diary that has been written from the special point of view of the individual's religious progress. This is true in general of the spiritual journals that have been common among the Quakers since the seventeenth century. It was certainly true of the vivid and voluminous diaries kept by John Wesley.* The characteristic of these diaries, however, is that their primary content as well as the purpose behind their being recorded at all was contained within a single doctrinal symbol.

For Wesley, as for the Quaker journals, the relation between God and man as expressed in the religious strivings and especially in the religious conflicts of their time, constituted the background of all that they encountered. This ongoing personal relation with God which they experienced was inherently a symbolic rela-

---

* See the Journal of the Reverend John Wesley, M.A., edited by Nehemiah Curnock, The Epworth Press, London, 1938.

tionship, the meaning of which depended on the general context of Protestant Christianity in its formative period of strength and upheaval. Wesley, like George Fox,* felt this symbolic relationship to be the most vivid and immediate reality of his existence. In his diaries, as in his life, he was primarily concerned with explaining and validating to himself his encounters and uncertainties with respect to it. His diaries thus describe his see-sawing relationship with God in the symbolic form in which God was real to him. Now he was in divine favor; now he was out of it; now he was back in it again, and a greater truth than ever before was being disclosed to him.

Such journals in their spontaneous intensity reveal a strong quality of personal authenticity. They are fundamentally different from a psychological workbook, however, with respect to their relation to religious symbols. The journals were carried out in terms of a symbolic assumption regarding the nature of religious reality that was not subject to question. The truth of the underlying symbol was part of the common sense of their culture; and their journals were the stories of their trials and pitfalls in coming close to this particular religious truth.

In contrast to this, the keeping of a psychological workbook involves no assumption, neither stated assumptions nor hidden and implicit ones, about the nature of reality and truth. To discover this, each in his

* The Journal of George Fox, E. P. Dutton & Co., N.Y. Everyman reprint 1948; introduction by Rufus Jones.

own symbolic terms and validated by his personal experience, is the goal behind the entire process and program of personal growth. Unlike spiritual journals, then, psychological workbooks do not begin by assuming intellectually that any particular structure of symbols is more nearly true than any other set of symbols. In the workbook, rather, the individual undertakes to achieve a personal contact with reality by means of the symbols and images that are brought forth from the depths of his psyche. His goal is to enlarge the scope and sensitivity of his confrontation with symbols in their endless variety and to reach by means of them more deeply into their many levels of meaning.

The essential difference between spiritual journals and psychological workbooks lies in the fact that the disciplines of depth psychology do not depend on postulating the exclusive truth of any symbol or doctrine. As psychological disciplines, they do not require and they do not lead to an act of faith or belief in any particular symbol. They lead, rather, to an experience, or series of experiences, by which the dimension of symbols as a whole opens to the individual and its inner principle becomes accessible to him. As his awareness of what is involved in this deepens, he becomes capable of recognizing the symbolic style by which reality reflects itself in the perceptions and life experiences of persons.

The psychological workbook is a valuable tool when used in the right way and at the proper point in the development of the individual. Its timing and context, however, are especially important. It does no good for an individual arbitrarily to decide that he thinks he would now like to keep a psychological workbook. It can only be used fruitfully if the commitment to maintain the workbook is authentically connected to a process of personal growth that is already well under way. Only then will the commitment to do it be strong enough to enforce itself in a disciplined manner over a sufficiently long period of time.

The best way for a psychological workbook to be used is in conjunction with face-to-face consultation in a depth dialogue relationship. It then serves to keep the contact vivid in the interim days between dialogue sessions. The act of maintaining the workbook serves to stimulate the movement of imagery material in the depths of the psyche; and it draws together the subjects and symbols that need to be discussed and extended in the sessions.

The dialogue relationship provides the best situation in which the individual can devise the style and format for a psychological workbook that will be most appropriate and fruitful for him. There are persons, for example, for whom poetry, painting, or music composition are important components of the workbook because of their particular talents and temperament. To have learned to keep the workbook as a continuing discipline is especially important, however, at the point where the dialogue relationship is coming to a close and the individual is preparing to carry on the work of personal growth alone. The workbook then becomes the main channel for continuity in the development of the person. It is at this point, also, that the third step in the program becomes important: to participate in group workshops where the individual can share his experiences with others and draw them forward in a social context.

GROUP WORKSHOPS

These group workshops are indeed workshops in the particular sense of being the place where the craftsman's work of fashioning a new image of personality is carried out. This is often difficult work, with much trial and error, tension and frustration to be expected. Egos jar against one another in the group, but the goal, and often the ultimate result of the meetings, is to neutralize the egos so that a larger-than-personal awareness can come forth.

The group quality of the workshops is of great importance. It provides a balance for the aloneness that is inherent in keeping a psychological workbook, and it is a valuable extension of the dialogue relationship. The group situation should not be misunderstood, however, as a place to practice sociability. The goal of the sessions is by no means to build an *esprit de corps* among the group nor to cultivate good fellowship, nor even good "interpersonal" relations. It is not infrequent that lasting friendships do emerge from them, but the group workshops are not a social meeting place. They are rather an opportunity for persons to meet others in the deep place of the psyche where they can enlarge the vistas of their experience.

This meeting in the deep place of the psyche is brought about by the atmosphere of the group situation. Great care must be taken in establishing it and in cultivating it throughout. Whenever possible, the group should meet sitting in a circle with all the members facing one another. Often, too, it is helpful to start the group sessions with a silence, or to have a period of silence after a brief, suggestive introduction. The introductory talk is to set the tone with which the participants in the group can relate to one another.

As the group settles in its circle and begins to come together psychologically, the tone that is established draws the focus of awareness away from the superficial aspects of individuality toward the elemental depths of the psyche. Attention is directed, then, not to the special and distinctive qualities of the others present, not to their unique personal styles, the color of their hair, the features of their faces, their accents of speech, their national or racial backgrounds, but to the core of essential humanness which is more fundamental than subjective differences. This unconditioned ground of personal existence, which the author of *The Cloud of Unknowing* calls, "naked being," is the deep place in the psyche where the group meets.

Once this ground of meeting has been established, so that it becomes a group of persons meeting on the non-individual level of the inward place, the major business of the workshop can get under way. The effect of this atmosphere is to neutralize feelings of separateness and subjectivity. Self-consciousness drops away, and if one has a private axe to grind, it somehow becomes irrelevant and unnecessary. One does not feel the need to insist upon that point of doctrine or of intellect which would otherwise have seemed to be of great importance. The persons who are present become free to drop the guards of individuality. They can enter the flow of the group at the depth where its movement is taking place. They are carried by it and become spontaneously able to share the elemental symbolic experiences of one another. An interpenetration of psychic depths takes place, unobtrusively and without being planned, but simply because the proper atmosphere has been established and a way has been opened for it.

It becomes possible then to share and extend in the group a variety of personal encounters in which individuals have felt that something basic within them has been touched and brought to life. They describe what happened to them, and the process of retelling kindles new experiences in others. As these experiences are shared without being inhibited by self-conscious analysis, they serve to evoke a fuller expression of ultimate concerns in all the group.

An example of what transpires in such a session is the description by a man who is a chemist of his experience in observing the leaves on the trees in autumn. He told the group how he suddenly realized that a moving unity is present beneath the surface of the colors, and that he himself was somehow connected to this unity. He told also the surprise with which he realized that he was not analyzing the changing colors in terms of their pigments, as his intellectual habits as a chemist would normally incline him to do. Instead, he found himself to be *feeling* the colors in terms of what he referred to as intuition. He described his experience as an enlarged awareness that lasted just a moment but carried with it a heightened sense of personal identity that stayed with him and was reawakened even as he spoke of it.

Stimulated by this in the session, an airplane pilot then recalled his own experience of feeling himself connected to his airplane not only as though it were an extension of his body, but as though they both were part of a greater unity that encompassed the air in which they were flying. Feeling this, he said, had the practical effect of enabling him to make difficult maneuvers with unusual intuitive accuracy; and it had the larger effect of connecting him to the more-than-human aspects of the cosmos by an intense experience of direct knowing. Hearing the chemist tell of how he had found a sense of unity through the leaves freed the pilot to tell his own subjective experience. He could permit himself to feel it again and respond to its implications. Then the group could share it with him, work with it, and further deepen the atmosphere of the inward place in which they were meeting.

In this connection we should note that one of the important functions of the group workshop is to free persons to feel and to tell their inward experiences. One of the psychological consequences of the modern attitude of matter-of-fact objectivity is that it leads people to repress whatever intimations of spiritual life may come to them. The heritage of materialism is that it causes people to feel shy about their personal encounters with larger meaning. Often people feel ashamed of such experiences, and ashamed of themselves for having them, as though it were an indication of illness, or at least of eccentricity. Thus the modern person is frequently in the position of repressing the memory of precisely those experiences that have the capacity of drawing him into contact with what is real in human existence. In the group workshops, however, an atmosphere is provided in which these experiences are affirmed. The individual is then encouraged to reach into the dimension of symbols and to develop the sensitivities of spiritual awareness in whatever terms they may come to him. Thus the connection of the chemist to the changing colors of the leaves, and the unity of the pilot with his plane in flight.

Another instance of what transpires in a workshop

session is a woman writer in the group recalling her dark moment when failure in her work and in her personal relations simultaneously descended upon her. She told the group of her isolation at that moment, not having even a conception of a god upon whose name she could call. The sense of being cut off from life deepened in her until she heard herself praying in phrases that were not her own. It was as though someone else were speaking. It was one of those spontaneous prayers that prays itself and finds its answer because it comes forth from the depth of the psyche. A new quality of consciousness then opened in her and reversed the downward trend of her life.

The group could enter an experience of that kind, identify with it, and explore its possibilities as well as its religious implications. In a similar way, they could participate in the emotions of a young woman who told of the first waking image of which she had become aware, the image of a butterfly flying in the midst of a crowded and busy midtown street. The butterfly was confused, but it seemed to be finding its way upward beyond the bustling people to a place where it could move in freedom. The members of the group were able to enter this image. They could share and support the feelings of personal transformation and new strength which the symbol carried. They could extend it also with images of their own, as the dream image of a housewife who saw the walls enclosing her life break apart and open a vision of effulgence beyond them; and

they could extend it with dreams and imagery like
that of Mr. Hart pressing on the locked door until a
mysterious hand came from behind him and opened it
for him in a mysterious way.

Each of these experiences is exceedingly personal
and subjective in its symbols. Their content is so private
and intimately related to the individual to whom the
encounter has come that it hardly seems possible for a
person to speak of it, much less communicate it in public. Nevertheless it is possible to communicate it. In fact,
a very important development in consciousness takes
place at the point where a person realizes that his basic
experience of contact with life, involving as it does his
intimate uniqueness, does not set him apart from others
but, rather, connects him. He can learn then that the
meaning of seemingly subjective experiences is not to
create barriers but to provide a bridge between persons. These experiences comprise a connective tunnel
that goes from person to person in the depths of the psyche. When an individual realizes that he can speak of
his private symbolic encounters and have them ac-
knowledged by his fellow man with a glow of recognition, something wonderful opens in him. The problem,
however, is how the point can be reached in a group
situation where one can speak and share these most intimate symbolic things.

It takes time, but the problem can be solved. It is, indeed, one of the primary reasons for which group workshops are important: to make possible communication

between persons on subjects that do not permit direct rational verbalization.

It begins with frustration, necessarily so, for the individual is trying to describe an experience which he encountered originally in a non-verbal form. It was a symbolic experience, and it came to him on a non-rational level. It was an inward experience, but at the point where he has put it into words to communicate it to the group he has by that much made it external. He has performed an act of translation in the very act of telling it. The usual experience is to find that the attempt to communicate a symbolic experience fails because the person who hears it can only perceive it from the outside. He is then unable to recognize the inner nature of the event that originally transpired in the psyche of his friend. This is why it is so important to develop an atmosphere in the group bit by bit, session by session, so that the persons participating in the group can reach an awareness of the reality that lies behind the words with which symbolic experiences are described. When you speak in the midst of such an atmosphere, you feel that the persons to whom you are speaking are not breaking into bits with their analytical habits of thought the things you are saying. You feel, rather, that they are reaching through the things you are saying to the very difficult, elusive experience that you are trying to express.

At such a point of development, an inward environment pervades the group. A meeting in the deep place of the psyche then truly becomes possible. In effect, the group workshops are arenas in which the varieties of symbolic experience can be placed on the center of the floor for all to see, so that the reality that lies behind these experiences can be felt, then shared, then entered into, explored, and extended. The outcome of this process over a period of time is that individuals cease to be caught in the web of doctrines and are no longer possessed by the particular form of symbolic experience that has happened to come to them. They are able then to see through the symbols and to reach through them to the reality of the encounter for which symbolic experiences are the vehicles. Symbols then become transparent to them, not because they have analyzed their meaning by one intellectual formula or another, but because they have perceived and appreciated the dimension of depth in the psyche within which the elemental symbols are truly real. In their transparency, the elemental symbols are indeed man's primary means of connection to the boundlessness of reality. To know this as a person means to become free and capable of reaching into the depths of oneself to glimpse the infinite imagery of life. In the group it means to share this dimension of experience with others through an interpenetration of the psychic depths, traveling by the vehicle of symbols. As one person enters the deep experiences of another, he is no longer concerned with the boundaries of self. His consciousness then extends beyond himself on that dimension of the psyche that overlaps the boundaries of persons.

Levels of awareness of this quality represent the fulfillment of group workshops in their advanced stages. Obviously they cannot begin on such a level, and simpler procedures are necessary to establish the preliminary atmosphere and to orient those who have not yet had direct contact with the process of symbolic unfoldment. In the earlier stages of group workshops, special texts may be used to achieve a familiarity with symbolic materials. Eventually, when the proper atmosphere has been established, the primary content of the sessions will not be drawn from the external sources of volumes of collected myths and wisdom literature. They will then be drawn rather from inward sources, from the life experiences of the members of the group; but before that is possible a considerable work of development must be done.

Fairy tales and myths can be especially helpful in drawing the group onto the symbolic dimension.* It is usually best, however, for the leader not to announce in advance the story or text that is to be used in the session. The most evocative effect seems to be achieved if the text is simply read by the group leader without warning so that a spontaneous response can be brought forth. Often, if the participants in the group know in

* See bibliography on p. 227 for a listing of books that can be used as resources and as starting points for group workshops.

advance what text is to be discussed, they will oblig-
ingly prepare themselves by reading it at home; and
once they have done that, if they are still new at the
work, it is very difficult for them to avoid intellectualiz-
ing their responses to it in advance of the session. The
session will then unavoidably become involved in opin-
ionizing that will make it very difficult for the group to
re-establish its ground of meeting on a deep level.

For this reason it is usually best to use shorter texts
that can be read in ten or fifteen minutes at the start of
the session, rather than longer ones which have to be
assigned and read in advance. It must be remembered,
however, that the use of tales and stories has purely an
introductory role in the group workshops. It belongs to
the early stages of the work when the members of the
group still require more exposure to symbols before they
can feel truly comfortable and at home with them. As a
person becomes increasingly relaxed and responsive to
the dimension of symbols, the tone of his relation to
reality changes. It softens, becomes more flexible, and
the individuals in the group are able then to be open
and sensitive to one another, as Martin Buber would
say, with total "unreserve." At this point it is no longer
necessary to use books as an external source of stimula-
tion, for the depths of the psyche of those participating
in the workshops have become the chief resource. Dialogue in depth becomes possible then, not merely between two persons meeting in private, but it multiplies

among many together who have entered the sacred place which is the depth of man.

This opening of connection among persons is a culminating experience which becomes itself the starting point for a larger relation to reality as a whole. It is the foundation of the transformed atmosphere of mind which must be socially established for modern man so that he can encounter reality anew with larger dimensions of awareness. This is the atmosphere which our time requires.

We must keep in mind, however, that this atmosphere cannot be achieved by being in favor of it, nor by pointing out how necessary it is. It requires a commitment to an active program of individual discipline by which the capacities of personality are extended in a way that actually brings about a larger experience of reality. If this is achieved for the individual in sufficient depth and numbers, it will eventually alter the quality of consciousness in the civilization as a whole.

The program for this may be applied with many variations and extensions, but its three essentials are: participation in a dialogue relationship with a second person who acts as evoker and guide in the development of the psyche; the maintenance of a psychological workbook which focuses and embodies the lonely work necessary for personal growth; and involvement in the multiple dialogue of a group workshop.

These three disciplines, taken together, comprise a

program for evoking the potentialities of man with respect to the "inward oracle" which is each person's private source of elemental truth; and with respect to enlarging the faculties with which this dormant knowledge of life can be aroused. In this sense the psychological way of reaching toward reality fulfills the ideal of Socrates. He also sought to solve a crisis in civilization by enlarging the capacities of knowledge in his fellow men. Where the discourses of philosophy were not sufficient, however, a program of personal disciplines based upon a psychological methodology may have a greater possibility of success. In any case, no doctrinal faith or organizational allegiance is necessary for the work of personal growth to be begun. It requires only the individual person and his willingness to inquire whether a larger dimension of reality than he has lived with before can reveal itself to him from the depths of his own existence.

6 The symbolic and the real

In the program of personal growth of which we have
spoken, keeping the psychological workbook is the link
that holds the process together. In whatever form or
variation it is kept, the workbook plays the unifying
role. It connects the dialogue relationship with participation in the group workshops, and with all other in-
volvements that are part of the deepening awareness of
the individual. The workbook is important because it
embodies the continuity of development in the person
through all the moments of frustration, insight, exalta-

tion, and especially of those periods of lassitude that intervene when the psyche seems to be in limbo. In these latter times, a person often feels that the momentum of life will never stir in him again; but the workbook provides a personal place in which he can struggle through the cycles that comprise the encompassing spiral of his existence.

The workbook is the hinge of the process because in it the individual records and re-experiences the inner continuity of his life. As he involves himself in the workbook, the process of inward growth establishes itself in his consciousness. It validates itself and becomes tangible for him. Increasingly, as he continues in the process, he feels the presence of the principle of wholeness working within him. This is the directing principle which is the essence of the psyche. It is a general principle, but as the individual experiences its manifestation, and as he recognizes its operation and its unfoldment in the midst of his life struggles, he feels the principle as his own. Though it is a universal principle, he experiences it intimately within him as "closer than hands and feet." This is the process in which personal realization emerges and is reinforced as a feeling of the integrity of one's own existence. When such an inward knowledge has established itself in the psyche, anxieties can be absorbed in the ongoing process of growth.

The development by which this becomes possible is embodied in the workbook over a period of time. It includes the varieties of psychological work. The process is carried on in private inward experience, and also at various points of contact with other persons, with a single individual in the dialogue relationship, and with many in the group workshops. All of these styles of relationship in psychological work may be engaged in together, overlapping in time. There is no necessary chronological order in which an individual should undertake the various aspects of the program. It depends upon personal circumstances. Any one of the ways may serve as the point of entry by which a sensitivity to the depth of oneself may be awakened. Ultimately all the steps must be traversed, but the process can be initiated from any starting point.

The question of what one is to do and how one is to do it is important; but after a while, when one has gained perspective, it becomes clear that the crucial question is neither what nor how but *where* the work is taking place. In this context, *where* means, at what level of depth in the psyche the personality is focused. In the dialogue relationship, for example, it is not nearly so important that any prescribed subjects be discussed as that the two persons meet at the very depth of each other and engage each other there. Similarly, in maintaining the workbook, the purpose is not to keep a scrupulous record of the goings and comings of daily life. The purpose of the workbook is to give the individual a tangible procedure by which he can enter the depth of himself and regularly re-experience his existence from an inward point of view. The workshops also do not depend for their success on the topics that are talked about. What is of the greatest importance is the *place* where the group comes together; and this place of meeting is the psychic depths of all who participate.

Going to this place in the psyche in a disciplined way is the key to the methodology of personal growth. The primary task is to become capable of going there; and for this it is necessary to develop a sensitivity to the symbolic style that characterizes the depth dimension of the psyche. Further, one must become attuned to its dynamic ways of operation, its principles and its paradoxes. Attaining this, recognitions of larger dimensions of reality may come and express themselves spontaneously and creatively—and sometimes surprisingly —in the course of a person's life. For the individual, this is the promise and pattern that lies behind the program of personal growth; but for the community as a whole, commitment to the goal of developing the inward sensitivity of persons means a transformation in the atmosphere by which reality is perceived and approached throughout the culture.

The nature of this dimension of reality is most clearly seen in the workshops, perhaps because the presence of a group provides a certain objectivity compared to the more private encounters. Consider, for example, the following type of occurrence which is frequent in groups. An individual tells an experience by which he was brought more closely and meaningfully into relation to life. It may have been cast in doctrinal terms, religious or philosophical, or it may have been totally non-doctrinal, as spontaneous imagery, like the experience of open vision beneath the earth, or the entry into the open spaces of the stone.*

In either case, whether doctrinal or not, his experience would have transpired in a symbolic context that could not be shared by all the other members of the group. They could join with him nonetheless, and they would do so by readjusting their focus of attention. They would move away from their individual habits of thought to the depth ground, the level of *naked being* in themselves, where they could affirm and enter the experience without understanding it intellectually.

At that point, the particular *form* of the experience is neutralized in the group. Its content and rational meaning become secondary, and a primary power enters the situation. At such a time, a spontaneous silence comes about, and the atmosphere often becomes so strong that it is felt as a tangible thing, as though it could be touched. It has the quality of "presence." But it has no specific terms, and there are no specific symbols by which it has been reached. It is as though all are meeting in the same *place*, but each has come there by his private road of imagery. Those present do not know and cannot know the inner content of one another's experiences. They cannot even know the quality of the experiences, nor their tone, nor their style. They may be similar to their own experiences, and they may only

* See Chapter IV.

seem to be; but that does not matter at all. It is not a barrier. The group recognition is not a question of content but of *where* in the psyche the experience took place. Then there comes a sense of all being in one place, which is not an outward place and not even an inward place, but a spaceless place. There is a perception of a unifying presence and of a meeting through diversity in depth on an encompassing dimension of reality.

There is epitomized here a principle that expresses the essence of religious truth. It is particularly pertinent in our time of history. This is the recognition that the reality of spirit as the power behind religious experience does not depend upon the specific content of rational doctrines believed as truths. On the contrary, the reality of spirit moves more fluidly and more profoundly without doctrines. It loses its vitality when it is hardened into fixed forms.

During the past few centuries in Western civilization, the interest in studying old religious dogmas by the dry light of reason has led increasingly to the tendency to think in black and white terms. According to this point of view, religious statements either are true or they are not true. To many persons, impatient with the doctrines against which they had felt the need to revolt, the only way the issue can be put is this: either there is a personal god or there is not; either there is a heaven or there is not.

More recently, harking back to older "mystery" traditions, there has been an increasing tendency to challenge the literalist approach to religion and to suggest that the Bible is best interpreted symbolically. The great conceptions of human destiny which were once viewed as sacred truth, as being literally the "word of God," are then described as a veiled wisdom, a secret doctrine to be opened by special esoteric insight. And this approach has indeed reaped a rich harvest in deepened awareness, especially during the past generation. Drawing upon a variety of ancient sources for its symbolic interpretations, it has extended the range of spiritual understanding and done much to modify the rigid thought patterns prevalent in a materialist age. For many people, however, the symbolic approach to religion retains an unsatisfying ambiguity because they never feel certain as to what is true and what is not true. They can appreciate, for example, that the doctrine concerning Heaven is a symbolic teaching; but is there, they want to know, an after-life, or is there not!

When the question is carried to its ultimate contrast in this way, we can see that the choice is finally not between a literalist and a symbolist point of view. The very statement of the question, the choice that it implies, is too narrow and must be transcended not only intellectually but by a larger experience of the dimensions of reality.

The varieties of depth experience which we have discussed, in the dialogue relationship, in twilight imagery, and in the workshops, all indicate that beyond the symbols there is a dimension of reality which does not depend upon the symbols at all but rather uses them. It uses the symbols as vehicles by which it enters and moves about in the world. It uses symbols as media through which it can unfold its latent meanings and participate in the lives of persons.

This, we can see, is indeed a larger dimension of symbolism, one that must be experienced to be known. One of the important functions of symbols is to point toward and to communicate insights and wisdoms of life that cannot be otherwise disclosed. This is the representational role of symbols, but it is not their major role. This is the role that the symbolic approach to religious truth has perceived and utilized, has indeed emphasized in its interpretations. But there is an additional meaning in the symbols that transcends the symbols themselves. It is the dimension of reality for which the symbols are vehicles, not vehicles for man but for reality itself, as reality manifests itself in the lives of men. Symbols in this sense are not merely means of communicating truth; they are embodiments of reality itself.

In this connection, there is a Hasidic story told by Martin Buber in his profound chronicle, "For the Sake of Heaven." * There the question is raised of what is the *way* that a person can follow in seeking truth and unity with God. The answer is given that this way is indeed like a road, but not a road that one walks upon. It is a road that one is in the act of constructing. Labori-

* Meridian, p. 62.

ously you roll the stones into place. You press them down. With much effort you roll the next one into place, and with great difficulty you smooth the tops, fill in the spaces between, and level it off so that it can be walked upon. You do it one stone at a time, and after a while you find that you have moved several yards forward. Working, you have been on the way. The road has come into being beneath your feet, for reality is not a symbol separate from you to be reverenced and interpreted. Reality, like man's relation to truth, grows as the tissue of his life.

In a similar vein, but with an additional point to make, there is the Islamic story of a pilgrim on the road to Mecca. He is traveling on his long and difficult journey bearing its many hardships, the privations of hunger and thirst, extremes of weather, the dangers of highwaymen. In the midst of his journey he finds himself thinking of how very long and difficult a journey it is. The sufferings he is enduring make him keenly aware that a great distance still remains to be traveled before he will reach the holy place of Mecca. Suddenly a light appears to him and a voice speaks to him upon the road saying, "Mecca is here, Mecca is now." The road he is traveling is the goal he is seeking. Mecca is the road, or more exactly, Mecca is the quality of the desire with which he travels the road.

The image of the holy city, be it Mecca or Jerusalem, is a symbol that represents the relation to what is real in human existence. To reach the holy city is, sym-

bolically, to have attained the point of ultimate realization. But to attain that level of awareness is not like an
object that one is given. It is not a physical thing to hold,
nor is it a doctrine in which to believe. Mecca is the
symbol acting itself out, unfolding in the course of the
journey. The symbol expresses the goal which directs
the course of action, but the goal is not separate from
the steps by which it is reached. It is integral with the
actions and with the quality of consciousness that permeates these acts. As the symbol unfolds, reality enters the world and becomes *present*. A new atmosphere
is established, and this is much more than a new cli-
mate of thought. It is reality increasing its presence
among mankind by means of symbolic events that are
enacted upon the depth dimension of the psyche. In another style of language, this type of event is often described as a breakthrough of *spirit*, into human experience. It has, indeed, all the traditional attributes of
spirit, for it possesses power, and meaning, and the
healing quality of inward peace. It expresses itself,
however, not in the fixed forms of dogma but in the
living fluidity of symbolic acts.

In this context, we can see that involvement in the
program of personal growth of which we have spoken is
not a means of reaching toward reality, but is itself an
act of participation in reality. To enter the place of
depth in oneself and to encourage actively the unfoldment of the elemental symbols in life is to increase the
presence of reality in the modern world. To engage ear-

nestly in a depth dialogue relationship, or to keep one's workbook, or to be part of a group workshop, is much more than a method of psychological development. It is an active involvement in that dimension of experience that channels reality into human life.

To participate actively in such work has the effect of making a symbolic Mecca, a sacred place, immediately present. In the act of doing the work that leads to the development of persons, the intimation of reality that is the driving image behind it makes reality present, just as Mecca becomes present in the midst of a pilgrim's journey. In this sense, too, wholeness of personality is not a goal that is off in the future; it is a condition of being that becomes present in the course of the work that seeks it. Likewise, peace is not an ideal that is off in the distance, but a quality of relationship that establishes itself at the depth of persons and creates an atmosphere where meeting can take place. Even more fundamental, the intimation of immortality which is so strong a yearning in man is no longer reduced to being an intellectual belief that must be projected into some nebulous world to come. Immortality becomes present, a condition of reality that is entered now, as the individual orients his existence to the dimension upon which the elemental symbols unfold. The validation of this lies in the continuity of symbolic experiences by which awareness opens in the depth of the psyche. In all the forms in which we engage in it, our striving as persons to touch and embody that which is real is the process by which the Real becomes present in the midst of our symbolic endeavors.

Ultimately man cannot know reality. He cannot define it, nor can he encompass it intellectually. To do that, his individual consciousness would have to be greater than reality, which is infinite. But he can work to make himself sensitive to it, and he can so attune himself to it that it will use his personality as a vehicle by which larger dimensions of meaning are expressed in the world. This is the primary role of the psyche as it draws meaning from the universe and mirrors it in elemental symbols which set the tone of social experience.

Working with the disciplines of the psyche, the modern person gains access to a dimension of awareness that transcends the dogmas of the past. The capacity to participate in reality through symbols can remake his existence because it liberates tremendous amounts of spiritual energy at the depth of the person. It fulfills a major spiritual role, and yet it is free from the metaphysical assumptions both of vitalism and materialism on which the conflict between traditional religion and secular culture has been based. The psychological way of depth experience provides a unitary path beyond metaphysics for, in it, the symbolic is the key to the real and becomes the vehicle for it.

Since it steps aside from the animistic conception of reality with which Biblical events are described, one might suppose that the psychological way involves a break with religious traditions. Quite the opposite is the case. The modern way of penetrating to the deep place of the psyche provides a means of re-establishing contact with the continuity of religious experience in past centuries so that the spirit behind those experiences can return to life and grow anew. The psychological way can achieve this because the insight it brings into the symbolic style of the psyche overcomes the literalism of traditional interpretations of the Bible. When the historical symbols are no longer opaque, one can look through them and recognize the breakthrough of the Real of which the Bible is a vehicle.

Knowing this, we can perceive the essential equivalence that exists between Biblical encounters with the spirit and modern depth experiences. Both are entries into the spaceless space of the psyche and touch reality there. When their common ground is understood, we can see that the ancient and the modern ways are two aspects of the symbolic unfoldment of a single abiding reality. Far from breaking with religious traditions, the psychological way brings a perspective and a methodology by which Biblical experience can extend itself and fulfill its promise in modern symbolic forms.

We can see the equivalence of ancient and modern experience if we ask ourselves what kind of event is taking place when a Biblical prophet states, "Thus sayeth the Lord God," and follows it with specific words and instructions that relate to the immediate needs of life in his time. It is a prophetic event in which the prophet as an individual has penetrated the depth dimension of the psyche, understanding it symbolically as the realm of the sacred. His experience emerges out of the context of the culture of the tribes of Israel, but it is an event of spiritual individuality. The prophet remains part of his tribe, loyal to and responsible for the needs of his culture, but in his moment of contact he is separated from it. He stands alone then, as Moses stood alone upon the mountain. There the prophet encounters a dimension of reality that becomes so intimate and personal that it speaks to him and discloses itself to him in the concrete form of images.

How can this abstract dimension become so intimate? By means of the intensity with which the prophet feels its reality within him. Entering the spaceless space in terms of his tribe's symbolic conception of the sacred, he goes further as an individual until he participates in the dimension of depth so intensely within himself that it expresses itself for him as a person-to-person dialogue with the divine. He recognizes it as this both symbolically and actually because he entered the experience with a firm awareness that this dimension of reality is one on which he authentically belongs. He felt secure in it, and confident that in his moment of need it would respond to his cry as though it were a person and would sustain him.

An experience of this prophetic type indicates the deep psychological atmosphere that underlies ancient Israelite experience. With it in the background, it became possible for certain individuals to know that there was present within them and accessible to them personally a dimension of reality that is valid in ultimate terms. When a person feels this so strongly that it becomes manifest to him in the concrete forms of images which can be seen and heard upon the dimension of depth in his psyche, a contact of transcendent power becomes part of his being. This is a major psychological fact of his existence. It then becomes possible for his life to become a connecting link between the dimension of depth, in whatever form its attributes may be symbolized in his culture, and the everyday world around him. Thus it is that the message communicated from the depth spontaneously translates itself into the phrases and the needs of the community around him.

From the psychological point of view, this encounter on the depth dimension takes place as though it were entirely within the individual; but also as though it transcended him. The literal concepts of inner and outer are not relevant here. The categories of space and time do not apply because another dimension of reality is involved. The experiences of the prophet are to be understood as being neither *within* him nor *beyond* him. They came *via* his psyche, his individuality serving as the vehicle by which a larger context of meaning could be brought into the world.

Meaning always enters the world in that way. It unfolds and extends itself in the course of history by moving in and through the lives of those sensitive psyches who reflect the cosmos at their depth and are able to translate its images into the words of the world. Reality grows and expands by means of such persons. They are the prophets and the poets who go to the highest and furthest mountain top that their culture and time in history permit. They find this highest mountain, paradoxically enough, in the spaceless space at the depth of the psyche.

In most civilizations prior to modern times, the primary openings of vision have come within a religious context of one kind or another, as the prophets and priests, the chamans and saviours speaking in the name of many gods. In modern civilization, however, the persons who become capable of reflecting the elementals of life very often do not function within the religious domain. They are linked to the continuity of religious experience not by a formal tie but by the common quality of sensitivity to the symbolic dimension. These are the artists, the poets, and playwrights, and above all, the creative scientists who reach out not merely toward knowledge of the physical world but toward a larger contact with the mystery of reality. These scientists include those who study the physical world, those who study the human spirit, and those scientists who work on the frontiers where the distinction between the physical and the spiritual has dissolved. They embody the creative thrust of intuition that is moving in the midst of materialism toward a new unitary experience of reality.

The starting point for the scientist is his attempt to

understand the data given to him in his particular field, physics, chemistry, anthropology, or whatever it may be. When he reaches the point where he is able to interpret this in a way that strikes a responsive chord of meaning within him, a recognition of especial strength comes to him. He senses then that he has touched something in the outer material that corresponds to an intimation of reality that he has felt within himself; and he feels it as a contact with the unity underlying life. Einstein has described this as a major factor in his personal experience, a reaching toward meaning in the universe which is finally fulfilled on the symbolic level in the research on which the scientist is working.

Prophets and poets, artists and scientists, those in whom the "inward oracle" spontaneously speaks, are the strong ones in a civilization. They are the ones who meet the problems of their time in a creative way. In the long run, however, the strength of a civilization does not depend upon the few individuals in the forefront, but upon the quality of persons in the community as a whole. This is why the program for personal growth of which we have spoken is especially important for the modern person who has no pretensions to prophecy or poetry but is aware of his role as a citizen of the world in which we live.

Each individual has the responsibility of drawing forth in himself the potentials of large awareness and of establishing a base of experience upon which his personal intimations of the infinity of life can unfold. As he develops his capacity to enter the depths of life through his psyche, and as his sensitivity to the symbolic dimension of reality grows, a new atmosphere will assert itself within his psyche; and from there it will radiate outward to influence others, even without conscious communication. When it is experienced by a sufficient number of persons who live as citizens of their time, the quality of personal being that it embodies will be felt as a *presence* in the community. Then we can hope to redirect the destructive course of history through transforming the mentality of man by disciplined involvement in the development of persons.

It is essential that many modern persons truly come to know that the human spirit is infinite, and that the forms in which it reaches toward reality are both symbolic and manifold. They must learn this not merely as a philosophy with which they agree intellectually, but as a fact which they have become capable of verifying repeatedly in their personal experience. They will know then why it is that if we place arbitrary limits upon the forms in which ultimate contact can be achieved, we are untrue to the magnitude of human personality.

One context in which this new perspective is especially important is our attitude toward the Bible. In the Biblical tradition there has been the view that when the Old Testament was finished and was certified in its standard version, that was the end of God's appearance to man. After that, man was not to expect a breakthrough of spirit in the world, at least not until the coming of the Messiah. All that was required of people, then, was that they repeat the formulas and the stories so that they would keep alive a remembrance of the great moments of contact with the divine which had taken place in history and were now restricted to the past. The traditional understanding was that since the voice of God stopped speaking when the Old Testament was closed, it would be best if people stopped listening for the voice of God in the world and concentrated on fulfilling the commandments.

When the experiences recorded in the New Testament transpired, this view was reconsidered and was opened anew. Then it was felt that God had indeed made a new entry into the world. Necessarily so, since He had needed to make a new covenant between Himself and man. With the ending of the experiences of the New Testament, however, the same tendency to restrain the human spirit and enclose it in fixed molds recurred. Again it was believed that the Spirit of God would no longer enter the world in a prophetic breakthrough. It would not, because it was no longer felt to be necessary. The truth had been given. After that it would be sufficient if people would *imitate* Christ and concentrate on entering the dimension of the sacred by repeating the tested formulas approved by the ecclesiastical authorities.

This is very reminiscent of the people who report in our group workshops that they had a deep and moving experience of contact several years earlier in their lives, but that they have not been able to repeat it. They keep on trying to do the same old thing and are disappointed to find that it never again has its original effect. These persons have to learn that encounters of the spirit are each unique unto themselves. The moment in which it first occurs and the form in which it occurs is the essence of the experience at that point of personal development. After that, one cannot repeat the same act of opening the same door in the same way again and again. There are other doors to be opened, each in a manner that meets the requirements of the moment in which it takes place. New contacts, new breakthroughs, will have the power of the original moment, but they must be new in form and new in content or they will not carry forward the process of symbolic unfoldment. Spontaneity is the essence of the opening of the spirit. When spontaneity departs, the old becomes regular and fixed and comfortable and hardened.

One of the very greatest and most basic difficulties in Western history is expressed in this fact, that we have drawn from our traditions a belief that major openings of the spirit are not possible any longer because they stopped when the Bible was officially sealed. We need to become capable of reopening the Bible as a living contact side by side with other styles of experience and sources of the spirit in the modern psyche. The two testaments which comprise the Bible are openings. They surely were not intended to be closings in man's relation to the infinite. Just because it is an authentic expression of the spiritual journey of man, the Bible is fluid and growing, as life is. We can see in its contents, as we could see in the individual experiences we have discussed in this book that the vehicles in which man's spiritual journey can be made are exceedingly variable. The number of their forms, like their source and goal, is inexhaustible.

In earlier times in the history of religion, the breakthroughs that transpired upon the dimension of depth in man were truly felt to be sacred. They were hallowed according to the symbolic style of their culture and they were regarded as transcendent. The belief in the transcendent quality of the divine is ubiquitous in the history of religion. It is a symbolic way of expressing man's intimation of the fact that the source of his inspiration is totally beyond him.

It may be beyond him, but in a special sense it is also within him. This is so because it takes place in spaceless space, the spaceless space into which we enter inexplicably, as Carl entered, while exploring the depths of the psyche. In their respective symbolic styles, primitive man and ancient man hallowed this ground of depth. In our day to hallow it in the old way is neither necessary nor possible. We are called upon, rather, to learn to enter the dimension of depth in our individual experience freely and by the light of modern knowledge.

The quality of the sacred will then become part of our existence, not as an object of worship but as an endless truth ever unfolding in our lives. With it we shall open a path by which fresh and continuing experiences of spirit breaking through the psyche will become increasingly familiar to modern man. Increasingly the modern person will feel at home on the dimension of spirit having found his way there integrally via the depths of his psyche. He will have forged out of his personal experience a new awareness of what spiritual reality is, not as an object of dogma but as the place of meeting in the depth of man where meaning unfolds.

☐ Bibliography

Allport, Gordon. *Becoming.* New Haven: Yale University
   Press; PB.
Apuleius, Lucius. *The Golden Ass.* (Tr. Robert Graves.)
   Baltimore: Penguin; PB.
Aron, Robert. *Jesus of Nazareth: The Hidden Years.* New
   York: Morrow, 1962.
Ballou, Robert (ed.) *The Bible of the World.* New York:
   Viking; PB.
Balzac, Honoré de. *Louis Lambert;*
   Seraphita;
* PB indicates that book is available in paperback reprint.

The Search for the Absolute;
Pere Goriot;
The Fatal Skin. Balzac's works are available in various editions.

Bergson, H. *The Two Sources of Morality and Religion.* New York: Doubleday (Anchor Books); PB.

Brinton, Howard. *Friends for 300 Years.* New York: Harper and Row, 1952.

Bronowski, J. *Science and Human Values.* New York: Harper and Row; PB.

Brown, Raphael (ed.) *The Little Flowers of St. Francis.* New York: Doubleday; Image; PB.

Buber, Martin. *To Hallow This Life.* (ed. Jacob Trapp.) New York: Harper and Row.
Tales of the Hasidism (2 vols.) New York: Schocken Books; PB.
For the Sake of Heaven. New York: World Publishing Co., Meridian; PB.
Between Man and Man. Boston: Beacon Press; PB.
I and Thou. New York: Scribner; PB.
Ten Rungs. New York: Schocken Books; PB.

Burton, Richard (tr.) *The Arabian Nights.* New York: Modern Library.

Carroll, Lewis. *Alice's Adventures in Wonderland.* Various editions.

Collier, John. *Indians of the Americas.* New York: New American Library; Mentor; PB.

Da Vinci, Leonardo. (Ed. Pamela Taylor.) *Notebooks of Leonardo da Vinci.* New York: New American Library; Mentor, PB.

Dostoyevsky, F. M. *The Devils (The Possessed).* Various editions.

Dubos, René. *The Dreams of Reason.* New York: Crowell-Collier; Collier; PB.

Eckhart, Meister. *A Modern Translation.* (Tr. R. B. Blakney.) New York: Harper and Row; PB.

Einstein, Albert. *Out Of My Later Years.* New York: Philosophical Library, 1950.

Eliade, M. *Birth and Rebirth.* New York: Harper and Row, 1959.

Cosmos and History. New York: Harper and Row, 1959; PB.

Myths, Dreams And Mysteries. New York: Harper and Row, 1960.

The Sacred and the Profane. (Harvest PB) New York: Harcourt Brace.

Fairy Tales. *Japanese Fairy Tales.* Mount Vernon: Peter Pauper Press.

Chinese Fairy Tales. Mount Vernon: Peter Pauper Press.

Russian Fairy Tales. Mount Vernon: Peter Pauper Press.

Yeats, W. B. *Irish Folk Stories and Fairy Tales.* New York: Grosset and Dunlap; Universal Library.

Robinson & Wilson. *Myths and Legends of all Nations.* New York; Bantam; PB.

De Angulo, Jaime. *Indian Tales.* New York: Hill and Wang; American Century; PB.

Fischer, Louis. *Gandhi.* New York: New American Library, Signet; PB.

Folk Tales: Tales Of Ancient India. (Tr. from Sanskrit by Van Buitenen. New York: Bantam Books, 1961.

Arberry, A. J. *Tales from The Masnavi.* London: George Allen & Unwin.

Fox, George. *The Journal Of George Fox.* New York: Dutton, Everyman edition.

Frank, Waldo. *The Rediscovery Of Man.* New York: Braziller, 1958.

Frankfort, Henri. *Before Philosophy.* Baltimore: Penguin; PB.

Freeman, Kathleen. *Ancilla to the Pre-Socratic Philosophies.* Oxford: Basil Blackwell, 1952.

French, R. M. *Way of the Pilgrim.* (Tr. from Russian.) New York: Harper and Row, 1962.

Gandhi, M. K. *Autobiography. The Story of my Experiments with Truth.* Washington, D.C.: Public Affairs Press, 1948.

Garrett, Eileen J. *Adventures in the Supernatural.* New York: Garrett Publ., 1949.

Gollancz, Victor. *Man and God.* Boston: Houghton Mifflin, 1951.

Ghiselin, Brewster. *The Creative Process.* New York: New American Library, Mentor, PB.

Graves, Robert. *Goodbye to all That.* New York: Doubleday, Anchor; PB.

The Greek Myths, Vols. I, II. Baltimore: Penguin; PB.

The White Goddess. New York: A. A. Knopf, Vintage; PB.

Herrigel, Eugen. *Zen in the Art of Archery.* New York: Pantheon, 1953.

Hesse, Herman. *Siddhartha.* New York: New Directions; PB.

Journey to the East. New York: Farrar, Straus and Cudahy, Noonday; PB.

Huxley, Aldous. *Grey Eminence.* New York: World Publishing Co., Meridian; PB.

The Devils of Loudon. New York: Harper and Row; PB.

James, William. *The Varieties of Religious Experience.* New York: New American Library, Mentor; PB.

Jung, C. G. *The Undiscovered Self.* Boston: Little Brown and Co., 1957.

    Answer to Job. New York: World Publishing Co., Meridian; PB.

    The Secret of the Golden Flower. London: Kegan Paul, Trench, Trubner & Co., Ltd., 1947.

    Psyche and Symbol. New York: Doubleday, Anchor; PB.

Kazantzakis, Nikos. *The Saviors of God.* New York: Simon & Schuster, 1960.

    Zorba the Greek. New York: Simon & Schuster; PB.

Keller, Helen. *My Religion.* Swedenborg Foundation, New York, 1927.

Kierkegaard, Soren. *The Prayers of Kierkegaard.* (ed. P. B. Le Febre.) Chicago: Univ. of Chicago Press, 1956.

    The Journals of Kierkegaard. New York: Harper and Row; PB.

    Fear and Trembling. New York: Doubleday, Anchor; PB.

Krutch, Joseph Wood. *The Measure of Man.* New York: Grosset and Dunlap, Universal; PB.

Lao Tse. *The Way of Life.* (Tr. Witter Bynner.) New York: Putnam, Capricorn; PB.

Levi, Carlo. *Christ Stopped at Eboli.* New York: New American Library; PB.

Lindbergh, Anne Morrow. *Gift from the Sea.* New York: New American Library, Signet; PB.

Melville, Herman. *Moby Dick.* Various editions.

Mercier, Vivian, and David H. Green. *1000 Years of Irish Prose.* New York: Grosset and Dunlap, Universal Library; PB.

Merton, Thomas. *The Secular Journal of Thomas Merton.* New York: Dell; PB.

Murphy, Gardner. *Human Potentialities*. New York: Basic Books, 1958.

Neumann, Erich. *Art and the Creative Unconscious*. New York: Pantheon Books, 1959.

Amor and Psyche. New York: Harper and Row; PB.

Nigg, Walter. *The Heretics*. New York: Alfred A. Knopf. 1962.

Pasternak, Boris. *Dr. Zhivago*. New York: New American Library, Signet; PB.

Patanjali, Bhagwan. *Aphorisms of Yoga*. London: Faber & Faber, Ltd., 1938.

Phillips, D. B. *The Choice is Always Ours*. Rindge, N. H.: R. R. Smith Pub., 1954.

Progoff, Ira. *The Cloud of Unknowing*. New York: Julian Press, 1957.

Depth Psychology and Modern Man. New York: Julian Press, 1959.

Death and Rebirth of Psychology. New York: Julian Press, 1956.

Jung's Psychology and its Social Meaning. New York: Grove Press, Evergreen; PB.

Radin, Paul. *Primitive Man as Philosopher*. New York: Dover; PB.

Reps, Paul. (ed.) *Zen Flesh, Zen Bones*. New York: Doubleday, Anchor; PB.

Ross, Nancy Wilson (ed.) *The World of Zen*. New York: Random House, 1960.

Scholem, Gershon, G. *Main Trends in Jewish Mysticism*. New York: Schocken; PB.

Schweitzer, Albert. *Out of My Life and Thought*. New York: New American Library, Mentor; PB.

Sinnott, Edmund. *Matter, Mind and Man*. New York: Harper and Row, 1957.

The Biology of the Spirit. New York: Viking; PB.

Sorokin, Pitirim. *The Crisis of Our Age.* New York: Dutton; PB.

The Reconstruction of Humanity. Boston: Beacon. 1948.

Stace, W. T. *The Teachings of the Mystics.* New York: New American Library; PB.

Strong, Mary (ed.) *Letters of the Scattered Brotherhood.* New York: Harper and Row, 1948.

Suzuki, D. T. *Mysticism: Christian and Buddhist.* New York: Crowell-Collier, Collier; PB.

Tagore, Rabindranath. *The Religion of Man.* Boston: Beacon; PB.

Gitanjali (Song Offerings). Introduction by W. B. Yeats. Boston: International Pocket Library; PB.

Taoism: The Text of Taoism. (Tr. James Legge.) Introduction by D. T. Suzuki. New York: Julian Press, 1959.

Teilhard de Chardin, Pierre. *The Divine Milieu.* New York: Harper and Row; PB.

The Phenomenon of Man. New York: Harper and Row; PB.

Thompson, Francis. *The Hound of Heaven.* Mount Vernon: Peter Pauper Press.

Tillich, Paul. *The Courage to be.* New Haven: Yale University Press; PB.

New Being. New York: Scribners; PB.

Dynamics of Faith. New York: Harper and Row; PB.

Tolstoy, Leo. *The Religious Writings of Tolstoy.* New York: Julian Press, 1960.

Toynbee, Arnold. *An Historian's Approach to Religion.* New York: Oxford, 1956.

Van der Post, Laurens. *Flamingo Feather.* New York: New American Library, Signet; PB.

Venture to the Interior. New York: Viking, Compass; PB.

The Heart of the Hunter. New York: William Morrow & Co., 1961.

Vining, Elizabeth F. *Friend of Life, the Biography of Rufus M. Jones.* Philadelphia: Lippincott, 1958.

Whyte, L. L. *Aspects of Form.* Bloomington: Indiana University Press, Midland; PB.

The Next Development in Man. New York: New American Library, Mentor; PB.

The Unconscious Before Freud. New York: Basic Books, 1960.

Woolman, John. *John Woolman's Journal.* New York: Corinth; PB.

Yeats, W. B. *The Autobiography of William Butler Yeats.* New York: Doubleday, Anchor, PB.

A Vision. New York: Macmillan; PB.

Collected Plays. New York: Macmillan, 1953.

Younghusband, Francis. *Modern Mystics.* London: John Murray, 1935.

Zimmer, Heinrich. *The King and the Corpse.* New York: Word Publishing Co., Meridian; PB.

Myth and Symbol in Indian Art and Civilization. New York: Harper and Row, PB.

Zohar. *The Book of Splendor.* (ed. G. G. Scholem) New York: Schocken Books, PB.

ABOUT THE AUTHOR

Both as critic of the old and as originator of new conceptions, Dr. Ira Progoff has long been in the vanguard of those who have worked toward a dynamic humanistic psychology. In his practice as therapist, in his books, as lecturer and group leader, as Bollingen Fellow, and as Director of the Institute for Research in Depth Psychology at the Graduate School of Drew University, he has conducted pioneer research and has developed major new techniques for the enlargement of human potential.

The core of Ira Progoff's theoretical work is contained in a trilogy of basic books. *The Death and Rebirth of Psychology* (1956) crystallizes the cumulative results of the work of the great historical figures in depth psychology and sets the foundation for a new psychology of personal growth. *Depth Psychology and Modern Man* (1959) presents the evolutionary and philosophical perspectives, and formulates basic concepts which make creative experience possible. *The Symbolic and the Real* (1963) pursues the practical and religious implications of these ideas and applies them in techniques and disciplines which individuals may use in their personal growth.

Basing himself on this trilogy of holistic psychology, in 1966 Dr. Progoff created the *Intensive Journal* concept and process as the means for making available to large numbers of people this method of furthering personal and spiritual growth. In 1971 he joined to it the practice of Process Meditation. In 1975 he published *At a Journal Workshop: the Basic Text and Guide for Using the Intensive Journal Process.* In 1979 its companion, *The Practice of Process Meditation* was a work in progress, nearing completion.

Dialogue House from its New York headquarters administers the national and international outreach of the Intensive Journal process.

Catalog

If you are interested in a list of fine Paperback
books, covering a wide range of subjects
and interests, send your name and address,
requesting your free catalog, to:

McGraw-Hill Paperbacks
1221 Avenue of Americas
New York, N.Y. 10020